Recommendation 666

Recommendation 666

✦

The Rise of the Beast From the Sea

Herbert L. Peters

iUniverse, Inc.

New York Lincoln Shanghai

Recommendation 666
The Rise of the Beast From the Sea

iUniverse, Inc.

For information address:
iUniverse, Inc.
2021 Pine Lake Road, Suite 100
Lincoln, NE 68512
www.iuniverse.com

All Scripture references are from the New American Standard Bible, unless otherwise noted.

ISBN: 0-595-28871-5 (pbk)
ISBN: 0-595-65919-5 (cloth)

Printed in the United States of America

**I dedicate this book to those
God gave the prophecies to—the honest doubters.**

*And now I have told you before it comes to pass, that when it
comes to pass, you may believe.*
John 14:29

Contents

Introduction

The events record in this book may, or may not, be actual fulfillments of Bible prophecy. At the time of writing, it's too early to know for certain.

However, even if it turns out that these fascinating events aren't the actual fulfillments of prophecy that I think they are, you will see how major prophecies could be fulfilled in your day—in real time—and nobody would even notice them.

Yet this shouldn't surprise us. After all, the Bible warns us that the day of the Lord will come upon the world like a thief in the night.

Now, I bet I know what you're thinking. This isn't the first time someone has written a book attempting to fit current events into Bible prophecy. So, before I begin, I want you to know why this book is different.

First of all, I'm not setting any dates. Jesus told His disciples: "It is not for you to know times or epochs which the Father has fixed by His own authority" (Acts 1:7).

Second, I'm not introducing a new way to interpret prophecy. On the contrary, I'm arguing that what reliable Bible prophecy scholars—such as Charles Ryrie, J. Dwight Pentecost, and John Walvoord—have long said would happen, has actually happened.

Third, I'm not forcing events into the prophecies. I've always strongly disagreed with those who do. I'm confident you will find that I have allowed the prophecies—and the events that appear to have fulfilled them—to speak for themselves.

Fourth, I'm not claiming to know who the Antichrist is. Although I do focus on an intriguing European leader, this doesn't mean he is the Antichrist. What I do believe, however, is that his powerful, new office in the European Union may soon belong to the Antichrist.

Now you're probably wondering where I'm going with this book. My goal is to show how the prophecies prove that the Bible is the Word of God. Only God could have revealed today's world events thousands of years in advance. It was prophecy that overcame my doubts and brought me to faith in Christ more than 30 years ago. And, watching these prophecies continue to be fulfilled today has caused me to marvel at God's sovereignty over the nations and the power of His unseen hand. This has tremendously increased my faith in Jesus and helped prepare me to be ready for His return.

My prayer is to share this experience with you.

PART I

Look among the nations! Observe!
Be astonished! Wonder!
Because I am doing something in your days—
You would not believe if you were told.[1]

      —God, between 650 B.C. and 330 B.C.

1

Joe Prophecy and His Six Misconceptions

If I had not received a phone call from Constance Cumbey, I probably wouldn't have had the courage to write this book. She called me at work and identified herself as an attorney from Detroit, Michigan. Since I own an insurance agency, I often receive phone calls from attorneys. So naturally I assumed she was calling about business.

"So what do you know about Javier Solana?" she said.

The question shocked me. I had been investigating this new European Union leader and his possible connection to Bible prophecy. I had also written about Javier Solana in some of the weekly religion columns I write for several newspapers. After Constance asked the question, I suddenly recognized her name.

"You're not Constance Cumbey the author, are you?" I asked.

"Yes," she answered. "I wrote *The Hidden Dangers of the Rainbow*."

Needless to say, for a small-town insurance agent her call came as quite a surprise. I had read her book—a No. 1 bestseller about the New Age movement—and still used it as a reference. Her excellent research was credited by many for blowing the lid off the New Age movement and exposing its existence to the world. But why was she calling me?

Constance said she was surfing the Internet when she ran across one of my newspaper columns. She had also been investigating Javier Solana and shared some of my concerns. Now I knew I wasn't alone. I finally knew someone other than myself who was arriving at some of the same conclusions about current events in Europe, and those specifically relating to Javier Solana.

So it was Constance's call that gave me the courage to write this book. Seeing the end-times prophecies being fulfilled may frighten some people, but it shouldn't. For believers, the fulfillment of these prophecies should bring great encouragement. For one thing, we already know how it all ends. For another, it assures us that the Bible is the Word of God and that our faith in Jesus has not been misplaced. But most importantly, it provides us with a way to reach the lost, unbelieving people all around us. At a time when science and philosophy have declared God dead, God is speaking to our skeptical world in a big way—by fulfilling His ancient prophecies.

This book is about events occurring in the Mediterranean and Europe that may indicate the end-times prophecies are soon to be fulfilled. One of these events occurred in Israel in 1992, and its significance has been overlooked. Now another major event may have occurred in Europe in 2000. And if these events are what I suspect—prophetic signs given as warnings to Israel—then the Antichrist is on his way and Christ's return is near.

Yet apocalyptic thinking of this kind is not easily accepted today. Right away, our mind goes to the bearded man on the street carrying a sign proclaiming, "The end is near." Many times people have predicted the end, and just as many times they've been wrong. This has left a bitter taste in people's mouths when it comes to Bible prophecy.

So, many Christians today have misconceptions about prophecy. As a result, they have stopped watching for the signs of Christ's return. Yet this was not the attitude of the early Christians. To these believers the Apostle Peter said, "And so we have the prophetic word made more sure, to which you do well to pay attention as to a lamp shinning in a dark place, until the day dawns and the morning star arises in your hearts" (2 Peter 1:19).

If the early Christians were advised to pay attention to the prophecies, then we should, all the more. The Lord's return is much closer today than it was then. And when He appears, it may be on a day we least expect.

Misconception 1: Everyone Who Studies Prophecy is a Screwball

When I first started writing newspaper religion columns, I went to a friend—the founder of a well-known ministry—for advice.

"Whatever you do, stay away from prophecy," he said. "You don't want people to think you're one of 'them.'"

"Them," of course, was a reference to all those people "we" don't want to be—the doomsayers, the kooks, the people with end-times Web sites written with large red letters and flames of fire.

But there is a problem with this kind of thinking. For one thing, Jesus gave us end-times prophecies, and then He commanded us to keep watching for their fulfillment (Luke 21:34–36, Matthew 24:42–51).

And someday these prophecies will actually begin to occur. And when they do, there will be people who notice. And, according to Jesus, these people will be dismissed as screwballs, just like Noah before the flood (Matthew 24:37–39).

The fact is, the Apostle Peter said that, in the last days, people would be turned off to Bible prophecy. He said, "Know this first of all, that in the last days mockers will come with their mocking, following after their own lusts, and saying, 'Where is the promise of His coming? For ever since the fathers fell asleep, all continues just as it was from the beginning of creation'" (2 Peter 3:3–4).

For there to be mockers, there first must be somebody to mock. And it appears to me that Peter is saying that the ones who will be mocked in the last days are the ones who are reading events in their time as possible fulfillments of prophecy.

Peter's words also imply that these last-days mockers won't only be nonbelievers. Mockers will rise up from among those who say they believe. Unfortunately, this is the way it is today. And it is in direct opposition to the Bible. The Psalmist says, "How blessed is the man who does not walk in the council of the wicked, nor stand in the path of sinners, nor sit in the seat of scoffers" (Psalms 1:1).

So, I believe signs may have occurred in the Mediterranean and Europe that indicate the beast of Revelation will soon be rising from the sea, but no one has noticed. This beast, of course, is the Antichrist and his kingdom.

But wait a minute. Before you think I'm just another screwball who is labeling some poor soul the Antichrist, you must realize this is not my intention. From the start, I want to make it clear: I do not claim to know who the Antichrist is. Instead, my book is about recent events that may indicate that the end-times prophecies will be soon fulfilled. I believe these events could be warning signs that the Antichrist is on his way.

Misconception 2: It's Always Wrong to Read Current Events into Prophecy

Christian history is filled with people who mistakenly interpreted events in their lifetime as fulfillments of the end-times Bible prophecies. In fact, many of the modern day Christian sects actually started around interpretations of prophecy that failed to come true. The truth is, much of the theology that now sets certain sects apart from the mainstream came about because of their leaders' need to explain why their predictions failed.

Some modern scholars actually suggest that this is the reason the New Testament book of Revelation was written. They believe the Apostle John wrote Revelation to explain why Jesus failed to return when expected by first-century believers. They point to the words of the Apostle Peter which seem to suggest he believed the end would come during the lifetime of first-century believers. He said, "The end of all things is at hand: therefore, be of sound judgment and sober spirit for the purpose of prayer (1 Peter 4:7).

Soon afterwards, "the end of all things," as Peter knew it, did come. The city of Jerusalem was destroyed, the Jewish nation ceased to exist, and the Jewish people were scattered among the nations. Jesus, however, didn't return.

From the time of the Apostles to the present day, people's interest in prophecy has had its highs and lows. When times were difficult and uncertain, interest in prophecy was high. And in good times, interest in prophecy was often low.

The rebirth of Israel in 1948 brought renewed interest in Bible prophecy in America. In 1970, a book on prophecy actually made the New York best-seller list and was named the No. 1 selling book of the decade. It was Hal Lindsey's, *The Late Great Planet Earth*. The Christian world once again got ready for Christ's glorious return to earth. Yet, like all those times before, Jesus didn't show up.

All through Christian history, we find similar stories of failed prophetic predictions. Many of them are tragic. And each time this story is repeated, another group of God's people experience great disillusionment and confusion.

It's no wonder we've arrived at a time in Christian history when—instead of flames revival—the subject of Bible prophecy can spark suspicion and skepticism. Yet this is not the first time many of God's people have had this attitude and have stopped watching for current events that could fulfill prophecy.

This was the same attitude many of Israel's spiritual leaders had when Jesus began his earthly ministry. Certainly this man was not the one the prophecies had foretold, they reasoned. After all, so many others had come before Him claiming to be Israel's long-awaited Messiah. In other words, Jesus came to Israel at a time when they least expected it.

Misconception 3: When it Happens, Our Christian Leaders Will Warn Us

As God has ordained signs to be associated with the change of seasons, He also has ordained signs to be associated with certain times prearranged in history. I'm reminded of what Jesus said to a group of religious leaders when they asked Him to show them a sign from heaven. He answered, "When it is evening, you say, 'It will be fair weather, for the sky is red.' And in the morning, 'There will be a storm today, for the sky is red and threatening.' Do you know how to discern the appearance of the sky, but cannot discern the signs of the times?" (Matthew 16:1–3).

Evidently, just as God has given us signs for the changing seasons, He has also provided us with "signs of the times." No doubt, as Jesus spoke to these religious leaders He was thinking about the many prophecies in the Scriptures that referred to Him. In fact, the prophet Daniel actually predicted the number of years that would pass until the coming of the Messiah (Daniel 9:25–26). Jesus rode a donkey into Jerusalem on that predetermined day.[2]

One wonders how the devout leadership of Israel could have missed these clear signs. Yet they did. It wasn't that they weren't watching for the signs; they were just looking for the wrong kind—something sensational. They asked Jesus to show them a sign from heaven when, in fact, He already was. He was fulfilling all the prophecies written about Him in the Old Testament before their eyes, in real time. In other words, the religious leaders in Jesus' day were looking for signs, but in the wrong places.

It's my fear that this may be happening today. Once again our world may be experiencing "signs of the times"—prophetic road signs warning about the return of Christ. And, once again, many of our spiritual leaders may be looking in the wrong places.

Misconception 4: When It Happens, We'll All Know

Have you ever started on a venture with a group of enthusiastic and like-minded people, only to be deserted by everyone before you finish? This describes the way I have come to feel about my quest into Bible prophecy. In the 1970s and 1980s, many Christians were very interested in Bible prophecy. For the most part, that interest was sparked by Hal Lindsey's bestseller *The Late Great Planet Earth*, first published in May 1970. Having survived the chaos and disillusionment of the

1960s, many in my generation began looking once again for something solid to believe in.

It was during this time of confusion that Hal Lindsey wrote his book. When I opened its cover, I found a quote taken from a documentary Lindsay had made. He said:

> I believe this generation is overlooking the most authentic voice of all, and that's the voice of the Hebrew prophets. They predicted that as man neared the end of history as we know it that there would be a precise pattern of events...And all of this would be around the most important sign of all—that is the Jews returning to the land of Israel after thousands of years of being dispersed.

When I read those words, Bible prophecy became more to me than just a casual interest—it became my salvation. You see, without Bible prophecy I would not have accepted the Bible as the Word of God. My logic was simple. If the prophecies in the Bible were true, then it was probable that the rest of the Bible was true. And the more I looked into the matter, the more I became convinced that the prophecies in the Bible were true.

Many in my generation came to the same conclusion. Books on prophecy began flooding Christian bookstores. *The Late Great Planet Earth* was made into a movie, and we all began looking for the "precise pattern of events" to occur in the Middle East and Europe that Hal Lindsey's book predicted.

But many years have passed since that time and, unfortunately, things have changed. Not many people are watching anymore. Why not?

I believe it's because many people misunderstood Hal Lindsey's purpose and became disillusioned when certain things didn't happen that he said might. What they didn't realize was that he was not attempting to predict the future; he was only suggesting possible future fulfillments that seemed to make sense. For example, when the European Common Market failed to become the foretold 10 kings of prophecy—as some understood Lindsey's book to suggest—many people lost interest in the subject.[3] The problem was that too many of us were focused on well-intended speculations and not on the Scriptures themselves. Then, when a 10-nation alliance actually appeared in Europe in 1995, no one noticed. (I will tell you more about this alliance later in this book.)

But for whatever reason, people turned off to Bible prophecy. They comforted themselves with the idea that, when these end-times signs occurred, they would know it. Why waste time watching?

But there is a problem with this reasoning. As I said, the Bible seems to indicate that the final events of history will actually occur at the very time when many have stopped watching. Referring to the second coming of Christ, the Apostle Paul says, "Let no one in anyway deceive you, for it (Christ's return) will not come unless the apostasy (falling away) comes first, and the man of lawlessness is revealed, the son of destruction" (2 Thessalonians 2:3).

Some believe these signs—including the apostasy and the revealing of the Antichrist—are only for Israel to see. They say these events will occur after the church has been raptured. Yet here the Apostle Paul wasn't writing to believers in Israel—he was writing to a new church in Europe (made up mostly of former pagans). For Paul to have assured this church that Christ would not return until after certain events, then he must have thought it was possible the church may witness them in some way—at least their beginning.

Besides, the Apostle Paul said the apostasy (or a falling away from the true faith) would come first. In other words, the apostasy would be on the scene before the Antichrist, not the other way around. This being the case, why should we think the church won't witness this falling away from the faith—at least its beginning?

Actually, as I said in Misconception No. 1, many Christians being turned off to Bible prophecy may be an indication that the great apostasy has already begun. The Apostle Peter said, "in the last days mockers will come with their mocking" (2 Peter 3:3). In other words, one indication that the end-times apostasy has begun is when those who believe in prophecy are mocked. And this is how it is today.

Some may argue that disinterest in Bible prophecy is not the same as falling away from the faith. I agree. But, when the watchman is not watching, the enemy will come. I believe this is why Jesus warned, "Therefore be on the alert, for you do not know which day your Lord is coming. But be sure of this, that if the head of the house had known at what time of the night the thief was coming, he would have been on the alert and would not have allowed his house to be broken into. For this reason you be ready too; for the Son of Man is coming at an hour when you do not think He will" (Matthew 24:42–44).

Misconception 5: Studying Prophecy Does More Harm than Good

We all like a good mystery. Perhaps this helps explain my interest in prophecy. Scattered between the pages of that old Book we find pieces of information about future events that have been left there by the Holy Spirit.

But the purpose of prophecy is not so God's people can predict the future. Its purpose is to strengthen their faith. To His disciples Jesus once said, "And now I have told you before it comes to pass, that when it comes to pass, you may believe" (John 14:29).

Yet, as I said before, some believe that studying prophecy is a waste of time. They even think it may be dangerous. These people point to the mistakes past Bible students have made when they tried to link current events with Scriptures. In their opinion, when these students of prophecy make a mistake, it does more harm than good.

So, in many evangelical circles today, the popular mood is that we need to spend more time winning the lost than speculating on prophecies. It's not that they don't believe in Bible prophecy; they just feel safer placing their attention on those things in Scripture where they believe they have a clearer understanding.

Actually, I can't argue with their logic. After all, we Christians are not here to bless the world by our charming presence, but to go out and declare the Gospel message of Jesus Christ everywhere we can. Yet here is where Bible prophecy can help. You see, if it weren't for Bible prophecy, I don't believe I would have ever accepted the Bible as the Word of God. And if the Bible is not the Word of God, then there is no good reason for anyone to believe in the Gospel of Jesus Christ.

Of course there are other reasons people have for believing the Bible is the Word of God. I have reasons other than prophecy now myself. But my point is that God gave us prophecy for a purpose. It is a powerful offensive weapon in our war against Satan's strongholds of darkness. Many people today are like I once was. Their minds have unknowingly been taken captive by the "Prince of the Power of the Air," and they've been imprisoned behind great walls of skepticism. Sometimes Bible prophecy is the only weapon that can breach those walls and set them free.

For example, I'm not qualified to stand up to a scientist and intelligently argue about evolution. I can, however, open my Bible to a passage of prophecy and point to its actual fulfillment in real-time history. In other words, if the Jewish prophets accurately predicted events thousands of years before they occurred, then I can argue that their message about the coming Messiah should also be considered.

Misconception 6: Christians Won't Be Here to See the Antichrist Anyway

This brings us to another common misconception. Many of today's prophecy students don't believe Christians will be around to see the rise of the Antichrist. This is mainly because they believe the rapture has to occur first. They say the Antichrist can't rise to power until after the restraining effect of the church has been removed. So, there's no point in Christians looking for signs they won't be here to see.

Although it may be true that we won't see the Antichrist's global power, we very well could be here to see his regional power. These students don't realize that the world's stage must first be set before the end-times actors can appear on the scene. And the world stage will take some time to be set. It is a common view that the tribulation period—the final seven-year period that precedes Christ's return to earth—will begin when the Antichrist signs a security agreement with Israel.[4] Many students don't stop to consider that—for the Antichrist to sign an agreement with Israel—the Antichrist and his kingdom must, to some degree, already be in place.

To set the world's stage for the end-times events, Israel must first return as a nation. Of course, this already happened. Then, after Israel has appeared, 10 nations in the geographic area of the old Roman Empire must unite in some kind of confederacy. After these nations have united, the Antichrist will come up from among them (Daniel 7:24). He will rise to rule over a revived form of the Roman Empire through deceit and false programs of peace. All these political events will take time to happen. And after these events have all happened, then the Antichrist will go and make his seven-year agreement with Israel (Daniel 9:27). In time, his kingdom will become global.

In other words, there's no good reason to think that Christians won't at least see the beginning of the rise of the Antichrist and his kingdom. We'll just need to know where to look. And the Bible points to the Mediterranean region.

It is commonly believed that the Antichrist will come from the Mediterranean area. Tim Lahaye, a Bible-prophecy scholar and co-author of the popular *Left Behind* series said, "One of the most frequently asked questions about the Antichrist concerns his nationality. Revelation 13:1 indicates that he 'rises up out of the sea,' meaning the sea of people around the Mediterranean."[5]

Jesus provided us with a few more details about the conditions that would spawn the Antichrist. He said:

> And there will be signs in sun and moon and stars, and upon the earth dismay among nations, in perplexity at the roaring of the sea and the waves, men fainting from fear and the expectation of the things which are coming upon the world; for the powers of the heavens will be shaken (Luke 21:25–26).

So, the Antichrist will rise from the restless sea of people surrounding the Mediterranean. This chaotic and stormy condition in Europe and the Mediterranean area will set the stage for the rise of the Antichrist. He will suddenly break on the scene with his ingenious solutions. Through deceit and false programs of peace, he will take power before the people who could stop him notice (Daniel 8:25).

And this, believe it or not, is the actual picture I've been watching.

Chapter 1 Notes

1. Habakkuk 1:5

2. J. Dwight Pentecost, *Things to Come* (Grand Rapids: Dunham Publishing Company, 1958) 246.

3. Hal Lindsay, *The Late Great Planet Earth* (Grand Rapids: Zondervan Publishing House, 1970) 85–6.

4. Tim Lahaye, *The Beginning of the End* (Wheaton: Tyndale House Publishers, 1972) 83.

5. Tim Lahaye, *Revelation: Illustrated and Made Plain* (Grand Rapids: Zondervan Publishing House, 1975 Edition) 172.

2

Eight Keys to Unlocking the Prophecies

Before I show you why I believe events are occurring that appear to be the fulfillment of end-times prophecies, I must first lay some groundwork. Even if you are already a student of prophecy and have an understanding of the subject, please keep reading. Sometimes it helps to see things from a different angle.

In my study of prophecy I have found several keys that have helped me in my understanding. I will share some of them with you.

Key 1: Keep it Simple, Student

When we study prophecy, we always come to the problem of interpretation. Who has it right? After all, those biblical images of beasts with many heads, horns and other strange body parts are difficult to understand.

The fact is, Bible prophecy is not easy. Without the right tools some of those images can be hard nuts to crack. Fortunately, with each one of those images, God has provided us with the right tool. Sometimes God gives us the interpretation Himself in a nearby passage. Other times He wants us to use the keys we have picked up along the way.

This brings us to our first problem. We try to make Bible prophecy even more complicated than it is. Think about it. The Old Testament book of Daniel is where we find some of the most amazing prophecies in Scripture. Yet, in Daniel, we also find a favorite children's story—Daniel in the lion's den.

My point is, God wants us to look at all those strange images He has given us just as a child would look at the pictures on a Sunday School flannel-graph board. I believe one reason God gave us so much prophecy in picture form was so we would look at these images like a child and expect a simple meaning.

In Tim Lahaye's book *The Beginning of the End*, he quotes David L. Cooper's "Golden Rule of Interpretation": "When the plain sense of Scripture makes common sense, seek no other sense, but take every word at its primary, literal meaning unless the facts of the immediate context clearly indicate otherwise."[1] So my first key to understanding Bible prophecy is "Keep it simple, student."

Key 2: Always Follow Prophecy's Morning Star

Our second key to remember is: "Always follow prophecy's morning star." And the morning star of Bible prophecy is Jesus. What do I mean by saying Jesus is our morning star?

Picture yourself in a dark world. Your only light is a bright star in the sky. As long as you keep walking in the direction of the star, you know you are headed the right way. This is the way Jesus helps us in our study of prophecy. He is both our guide and our goal.

The Apostle Peter said, "And so we have the prophetic word made more sure, to which you do well to pay attention as to a lamp shinning in a dark place, until the day dawns and the morning star arises in your hearts" (2 Peter 1:19).

This morning star Peter refers to is Jesus. We know this because of the last chapter of the book of Revelation. Jesus said to John, "I, Jesus, have sent My angel to testify to you these things for the churches. I am the root and the off-spring of David, the bright morning star" (Revelation 22:16).

What does Jesus mean? If our interpretations of Bible prophecy lead us away from a simple faith in Jesus, or away from the Jesus in the Bible, we are going off course.

In other words, we need to let Jesus guide us through our study of prophecy like a bright, morning star.

Key 3: Focus on Israel

Here we have an important key to unlocking the images of Bible prophecy—remember to focus on Israel. In prophecy, our geographical focus is always Israel. From God's point of view, Jerusalem is the center of the world. He said through Ezekiel, "This is Jerusalem; I have set her at the center of the nations, with lands around her" (Ezekiel 5:5).

God chose to work through the nation of Israel to reveal Himself to the world. The Bible we study, the promises we rely on for our salvation, and the Messiah who fulfilled those promises and purchased our salvation have all come through Israel.

John Walvoord, author of many books on Bible prophecy and former president of Dallas Theological Seminary, also believes the nation of Israel is an important key to understanding prophecy. In his book *The Nations in Prophecy*, Walvoord said:

> The biblical point of view, therefore, is quite different from that of the world in general to whom Israel was an insignificant people. From the standpoint of God's divine election, Israel is instead the key, and through Israel God was to fulfill His purpose whether redemptive, political, or eschatological.[2]

So Bible prophecy mainly deals with hard historical realities that have to do with Israel, the surrounding nations, and Israel's Messiah.

Key 4: Images in Prophecy Have an On-Going Nature

When you think about it, prophecy is just history. The only difference is, in Bible prophecy some of the history hasn't happened yet.

This brings us to another important key: Images in prophecy have an on-going nature. This is because God sees the end from the beginning at the same time. For example, we find a great, red, seven-headed dragon mentioned in the book of Revelation, the last book of the Bible. This dragon represents the way God sees Satan and the subjects he controls. In Genesis, the first book of the Bible, Satan is described as a serpent. Between the time of his first encounter with humankind in Eden, to his final defeat at the return of Christ, Satan will have grown into a great red dragon with seven heads. So, keep in mind that the images in prophecy have an on-going nature.

Key 5: Knowing the Old Is a Key to the New

The Word of God must been taken as a whole. The prophecies in the New Testament can't be correctly understood apart from the Old Testament.

I have already mentioned the example of the great, red dragon we find in the book of Revelation. To understand the meaning of this dragon, we have to go back to the book of Genesis where this dragon was just a little serpent.

Another example of how the Old Testament helps us interpret the New Testament prophecies comes from our understanding of who the "Babylon" is in Revelation. According to Revelation, Babylon will return to the world stage only to be destroyed in one hour with fire.

To understand who this Babylon of Revelation represents, it helps us to go back and read about where ancient Babylon had its beginning—at the Tower of Babel in Genesis 11. Here we read that the nations were created when God confused the languages of the builders of the Tower of Babel and scattered them across the earth. So, the Babylon we find in the book of Revelation may have something to do with these nations coming back together. I believe it may be the United Nations, and I will show you why later in this book.

Key 6: Nebuchadnezzar's Dream is Our Overlay

Sometimes one important key can open the way to many keys. A dream God gave to a pagan king is one of those keys.

The king was Nebuchadnezzar. But he wasn't just any king. This was Nebuchadnezzar the Great, the king of the vast Babylonian Empire.

The dream came to the king when he had been thinking about the future. He saw a huge statue shaped like a man. It had a head made of gold, a breast of silver, a belly of brass, legs of iron, and feet and toes of iron and clay. As the king was watching, a stone struck the statue at its feet and shattered it into dust. Then the stone grew to become a great mountain and filled all the earth (Daniel 2:31–35).

This dream provides us with many important keys to unlocking the strange images in prophecy. The reason for this is that God Himself provides us with the correct interpretation of the king's dream. This is a great help to us when we try to interpret the other images that follow.

The statue represents the four major Gentile kingdoms, beginning with Babylon, that will oppress the children of Israel before Christ comes the second time to establish His eternal kingdom. Jesus referred to the period of time represented by the statue as the "times of the Gentiles" (Luke 21:24). The stone that destroyed the statue and grew into a mountain represents the Messiah and His coming kingdom to Israel.

When we look at history, it's amazing to see how accurate the king's dream has already been. Through Daniel's interpretation, God tells Nebuchadnezzar that the different metals of the statue represent successive kingdoms. Daniel tells the king that he is the head of gold—representing the Babylonian Empire (Dan. 2:38). The silver arms and chest represent the less powerful Medo-Persian

Empire that followed the Babylonian Empire. The belly of brass represents the even more inferior Greek Empire. And the iron legs represent the Roman Empire.

It's commonly believed that the feet of iron and clay will be a revival of the old Roman Empire and that the toes will be a 10-nation alliance that will rule over it. In Part 2 of this book, I will show how this is currently happening with the nations coming together in the European Union.

The importance of King Nebuchadnezzar's dream, then, is that it gives us many keys to unlock the images that follow. God not only gives us the correct interpretation of these prophecies, but actual history can now be used to see how God fulfilled them.

This is helpful because these images from Daniel show up again in Revelation. We can use the image of the statue as an overlay to help us stay on the correct course when interpreting those prophecies. For example, since we know that the statue represents real earthly empires and their relationship to Israel, then we know that the coming kingdom of the Messiah will also be a real kingdom—the stone that becomes a mountain. So if our interpretation does not lead us to a literal restoration of God's promised kingdom to Israel, then we have gone wrong somewhere.

Key 7: Look at Things From God's Point of View

The king's dream also reveals to us that God is concerned and involved with our politics. Here we find God inflicting a king with dreams he can't understand. This tells us that God was concerned and involved with the politics in Babylon. This was because the politics in Babylon had an effect on God's plans for Israel.

For the same reason, God could well become involved in the politics of any nation, including America. In fact, I believe it would surprise us to know just how much God has been involved with our politics. The only reason we don't see it is because God doesn't always do what we expect Him to do.

This brings us to another important key: Look at things from God's point of view. This is because God sees things differently than we do. If you recall, in his dream the king saw a magnificent statue of a man. While he was watching, a stone struck the statue at its feet, destroyed it, and the stone became a huge mountain. God was revealing the future in a way this pagan king could especially appreciate. He was showing him what would happen to his kingdom and the kingdoms following his.

Yet, as I said, God sees things from a different angle than we do. Later God gave the prophet Daniel a dream about the same future. But God revealed it to His faithful servant in a different way—the way He saw things. Instead of showing Daniel a magnificent statue of a man to represent the four Gentile kingdoms, God showed Daniel four wild beasts rising from the sea.

The first beast Daniel saw was like a lion. This beast represented Babylon. The second resembled a bear. It represented Medo-Persia. The third was like a leopard and represented Greece. The fourth beast was not compared to any animal. It was different from all the other beasts—it had iron teeth and had ten horns. This beast represented Rome.

Some Bible students believe these four beasts Daniel saw rising from the sea represent different kingdoms than those Nebuchadnezzar saw in his dream. One reason is because later—when the fourth and last beast is destroyed—Daniel says of the other beasts that "an extension of life was granted them for an appointed period of time" (Daniel 7:12). These students reason that if these beasts represented the previous empires of Babylon, Medo-Persia and Greece, then it wouldn't be possible for them to be given an extension of life. After all, these empires ceased to exist a long time ago.

But I believe this opinion fails to take into consideration the on-going nature of these images of prophecy. In this passage where these beasts are granted an extension of life, they represent the people who remain from those Gentile kingdoms who are allowed into Christ's earthly kingdom at the end of the tribulation period (Matthew 25:31–46).

There is another indication that the beasts Daniel saw represent the same four kingdoms from Nebuchadnezzar's dream. It comes from his description of the first beast. Daniel wrote, "The first [beast] was like a lion and had the wings of an eagle. I kept looking until its wings were plucked, and it was lifted up from the ground and made to stand on two feet like a man; a human mind also was given to it" (Daniel 7:4).

To understand Daniel's statement, we need to use the keys we have learned so far. This lion Daniel saw rising from the sea represents Nebuchadnezzar from God's point of view. How can we know this? Once, to teach this proud king a lesson in humility, God actually gave Nebuchadnezzar the mind of a beast for seven years. When the seven years ended, the Bible tells us this king looked up and gave honor to God. After he humbled himself by acknowledging God's sovereignty, his human mind was returned to him. This is when, from God's point of view, this pagan beast-king was given the mind of a man. And this was the meaning of the first lion-like beast Daniel saw rising from the sea.

Remember, God sees things differently than we do. We see our leaders and our governments as things of grandeur and beauty, but God considers them unreasoning and dangerous beasts that need to be restrained.

Key 8: Follow the Road Signs

Perhaps one of the biggest mistakes we students of prophecy make is failing to recognize the difference between details and prophetic road signs. So my last key is: Follow the road signs. Although God has given us many amazing details of the future in the Bible, we must learn to recognize the difference between details and road signs. When we fail to follow the prophetic road signs, it's easy to get hung up in the details and go off course.

Prophetic road signs are events that were foretold in Scripture and are now documented in history. But, too many times, we focus on events that are questionable. For example, many students of prophecy believe one of the signs of the Lord's return is an increase in the frequency of earthquakes. For this reason, they are always drawing our attention to the latest count.

I believe they may be right. Yet an increase in the frequency of earthquakes is debatable because not all experts agree that they have increased. So I wouldn't classify recent earthquakes as prophetic road signs.

Yet, the rebirth of the nation Israel in 1948 was a prophetic road. It was foretold by the prophets and is now documented in history.

This doesn't mean everyone who sees a prophetic road sign will appreciate its prophetic meaning. It simply means everybody will agree that the event occurred. And by carefully following the prophetic road signs, we are more apt to stay on the right course.

I consider the Schuman Declaration another major prophetic road sign in history. On May 9, 1950, French Foreign Minister Robert Schuman presented his proposal that led to the creation of the European Coal and Steel Community—considered by Europeans to be the first step in the reunification of Europe. This date has now become a symbol of the European Union—like July Fourth is to America—and is known as Europe Day.

Although not everybody may recognize or agree with the prophetic implications, almost everybody realizes that Schuman's Declaration marked the beginning of the reunification of the nations of Europe that we are witnessing today. The appearance of the EURO in January 1999—the new single currency of the European Union—has convinced even some of the more skeptical that the nations of Europe are uniting. This revival of the Roman Empire was foretold by the prophets, and there is a recognized day in history when it began—Europe Day.

Think about it. What good is a prophecy if the event that fulfilled it is not established in history? This would not serve God's purpose for Bible prophecy. Beware of those who tell you certain Bible prophecies have been fulfilled without being able to point to reliable historical events as proof.

So remember, learn to recognize and follow the prophetic road signs before attempting to fill in the details.

Chapter 2 Notes

1. Tim Lahaye, dedication, *The Beginning of the End.*

2. John F. Walvoord, *The Nations in Prophecy* (Grand Rapids: Zondervan Publishing House, 1967) 52.

3

A Quick Look at Revelation

The Four Views

Now that we have a few simple keys to help us take some of the mystery out of Bible prophecy, let's take a quick look at the book of Revelation.

There are four basic views about how to interpret this difficult book. One is the spiritual view of interpretation. People who use this method don't take the book of Revelation literally. They believe the only purpose of Revelation is to teach fundamental spiritual truths that apply to the church throughout history. For example, it teaches believers to overcome and remain faithful to Christ in the midst of persecution.

Another view is the preterist view. According to this view, most of the prophecies of the book of Revelation were fulfilled in the first century during the Jewish War and destruction of the temple in A.D. 70. Therefore, they do not await future fulfillment.

The third is the historical view. People who hold to this interpretation believe the book of Revelation deals with the history of the church, from the first century to modern times. In other words, they believe the strange images and events described in Revelation are the experiences of the church as she goes through history.

The fourth is the futurist view. This is the belief that the book of Revelation contains prophecies that will be fulfilled in the end times. This is the way the people I've quoted in this book—Tim Lahaye, Clarence Larkin, H.L. Willmington, J. Dwight Pentecost, John Walvoord and Hal Lindsey—interpret the book of Revelation. This is also my view.

Yet because we believe the book of Revelation contains prophecies about future events, this doesn't mean we don't recognize the possibility of past applications. As we have learned in our study of the keys, these images in Bible prophecy have an on-going nature. This being the case, there is no reason some of these images found in Revelation couldn't have had meaning for God's people in different periods of history. This multiple application is clearly demonstrated in the Old Testament prophecies concerning Israel's coming Messiah.

And a good New Testament example of this multiple application comes from some words Jesus once said to His close disciples. As they were leaving the temple in Jerusalem, His disciples commented to Him about its beauty. At this time the Jewish temple was still under construction by King Herod. Herod was known far and wide for his marvelous stonework. Massive stones were not only intricately cut to fit tightly in place, but they were also beveled to enhance their beauty—even the foundation stones that wouldn't be seen.

Jesus answered His disciples by saying, "Do you not see all these stones? Truly I say to you, not one stone here shall be left upon another, which will not be torn down" (Matthew 24:2).

Here we have a prophecy that has already been fulfilled. Less than 40 years after Jesus made this prediction, Roman soldiers surrounded and besieged Jerusalem. When the battle was finally over, the destruction inflicted upon the city had been so complete that not one of Herod's beautiful stones was left upon another on the temple mount.

When Jesus made this prediction, His disciples wanted to know more. When they were alone with Him, they asked, "Tell us when will these things be, and what will be the sign of Your coming, and the end of the age?" (Matthew 24:3).

Whether they knew it or not, they were asking Him two questions. Their first question was regarding the destruction of the temple. Their second was regarding when Jesus would return from heaven to set up His earthly kingdom. So Jesus responded in a way that would answer both of these questions.

But this confronts us with a problem. How do we know which sign applies to which question? For example, when Jesus said, "Therefore, when you see the Abomination of Desolation which was spoken through Daniel the prophet, standing in the holy place (let the reader understand); then let those who are in Judea flee to the mountains" (Matthew 24:15–16). Was Jesus talking here about an event that would indicate the imminent destruction of the temple in A.D. 70, or His second coming?

Yet here is another beautiful example of how the Bible interprets itself. In the book of Luke, we find a parallel account of this incident. But here, the disciples only ask Jesus the first question. So in Luke, Jesus provides us with the answer to only the first question—the one regarding the destruction of the temple. His disciples only ask, "Teacher, when therefore will these things be? And what will be the sign when these things are about to take place?" (Luke 21:7). The only question here is about the destruction of the temple.

In answer to this more specific question, Jesus said, "But when you see Jerusalem surrounded by armies, then recognize that her desolation is at hand. Then let those who are in Judea flee to the mountains..." (Luke 21:20–21).

But in Matthew, where two questions were being asked, Jesus told them to flee to the mountains when they saw the Abomination of Desolation—not when they saw Jerusalem surrounded. In fact, Luke does not even mention something as important as the Abomination of Desolation.

We can infer from these two accounts that the sign Jesus provided His disciples for the destruction of the temple in A.D. 70 was when they saw Jerusalem surrounded by armies. And the sign He gave us that would precede His return to earth would be the appearance of the Abomination of Desolation in the rebuilt temple.

Back to my main point. Here in Matthew we find an example of how the same prophecies in the Bible can have a meaning for God's people at different periods in history and still be predictions about events that will occur in the end times. Now let's take a look at the book of Revelation.

The Three Parts

The entire book of Revelation is a message Jesus wanted the Apostle John to deliver to seven churches that existed at that time in Asia Minor (Revelation 1:11, 22:16).

The message to the churches was given to the Apostle John by visions. He didn't just hear the message; he also saw the message. It was broken up into three parts—the things John had just seen about Jesus, the things that are, and the things which shall take place after the things that are. Jesus said to John, "Write therefore the things which you have seen, and the things which are, and the things which shall take place after these things" (Revelation 1:19).

John had just seen Jesus standing in the middle of seven golden lampstands. But this Jesus didn't look the same as the one John had laid his head against (John 13:23). John said:

> I saw one like a son of man, clothed in a robe reaching to the feet, and girded across His chest with a golden sash. His head and His hair were white like wool, like snow: and His eyes were like a flame of fire. His feet where like burnished bronze, when it has been made to glow in a furnace, and His voice was like the sound of many waters. In His right hand He held seven stars, and out

of His mouth came a sharp two-edged sword: and His face was like the sun shining in its strength (Revelation 1:13–16).

It turned out the lampstands represented the seven churches Jesus wanted John to deliver this prophecy to. And the seven stars represented the seven angels of these seven churches. There's much debate over whether these stars represent real angels or human pastors of the churches. At this time, I'm still open on the matter.

Remember I told you the book of Revelation is broken into three parts—the things John saw, the things that are, and the things that take place after the things that are. Now let's move from the things John saw to the second part of Revelation—the things that are.

The "things that are" is the present age of the churches represented by the seven golden lampstands. Chapters 2 and 3 are letters to seven individual, first-century churches. Jesus praises them for what they are doing right and scolds them for what they are doing wrong.

Although Jesus had different things to say to each one of the churches, there was something He said to all seven. He warned them all to stay attentive to what the Holy Spirit had to say to the churches, and He encouraged them to overcome the world. For example, to the church at Ephesus Jesus said, "He who has an ear, let him hear what the Spirit says to the churches. To him who overcomes, I will grant to eat of the tree of life, which is in the Paradise of God" (Revelation 2:7).

You see, God didn't place these churches in Asia Minor without purpose. They were like lampstands against the darkness—they were actually holding something back. These churches each differed in their circumstances, but they had the same assignment—they were to overcome the world. The world referred to Satan and his influence over the kingdoms of earth.

It is evident from these letters that it's possible for a church to fail in its assigned mission. Jesus warned the church at Ephesus, "But this I have against you, that you have left your first love. Remember therefore from where you have fallen, and repent and do the deeds you did first; or else I am coming to you, and will remove your lampstand out of its place—unless you repent" (Revelation 2:4–5).

Fortunately, at this time, one church losing its lampstand did not represent the loss of all the churches. Although these early churches recognized the authority of the Apostles, at this time in Christian history they were still independent bodies (1 Thessalonians 2:14).

Unfortunately, by the time of the Roman Emperor Constantine, all seven of these churches were swallowed up by the Roman state superchurch. Yet, the concept of independent churches somehow managed to survive.

By "independent churches," I'm not referring to what we know today as non-denominational churches. And I don't believe there's anything wrong with churches that organize themselves into denominations either. What I mean by "independent" are what some refer to today as "free churches." They only recognize Christ and the teachings of the original Apostles, as found in the Bible, as their authority and not some earthly ecclesiastic order or system.[1]

After the Reformation, these independent churches would re-emerge as bright as ever. In fact, in my opinion, these independent churches are responsible for much of the blessings and freedoms we enjoy here in America. You see, I believe the effect these independent churches had was to reveal on earth what Jesus referred to as the "kingdom of heaven." There are different views concerning the meaning of the kingdom of heaven. You may wish to study the opinion of others on this subject.

Let me give you my opinion. I believe the kingdom of heaven can be understood as an extension of the power, authority and presence of Christ (1 Corinthians 2:4–5, 4:20, Revelation 3:8). The kingdom of heaven on earth actually had its beginning before the establishment of the church. It began with the preaching of John the Baptist (Matthew 11:11–14). You see, Jesus brought the kingdom of heaven with Him. And when people believed in Jesus, they began establishing His earthly kingdom. When Jesus was crucified and returned to heaven, His power, authority and presence continued on earth in His churches. In other words, today the earthly kingdom of heaven is an extension of the churches that make up His church.

The kingdom of heaven was first offered to Israel. So, when Israel rejected it, it was offered to the Gentile world. To Israel, Jesus said:

> Did you never read in the Scriptures, 'The stone which the builders rejected, this became the chief corner stone; this came about from the Lord, and it is marvelous in our eye'? Therefore I say to you, the kingdom of God will be taken away from you, and be given to a nation producing the fruit of it. And he who falls on this stone will be broken to pieces; but on whom ever it falls, it will shatter him like dust (Matthew 21:42–44).

So the kingdom of heaven was offered to the Gentile nations. It took root in Asia Minor with the seven churches. This is why Jesus sent them a message in the book of Revelation. He wanted them to understand their mission on earth and what would happen when they were gone.

The Apostle John already understood this. In a letter he had said, "For whatever is born of God overcomes the world; and this is the victory that has overcome the world—our faith. And who is the one who overcomes the world, but he who believes that Jesus is the Son of God" (1 John 5:4–5).

You see, when Jesus came to Israel, He stopped something. Satan's control over the world through his vast Roman Empire was overruled by a greater power—Jesus, the Son of God.

After Jesus was crucified and returned to heaven, He left His followers and the church behind in His place (John 17:11–26, 21:21–23, Matthew 28:16–20). The Apostle Paul realized the great power of the church. He said, "And He put all things in subjection under His (Christ's) feet, and gave Him (Christ) as head over all things to the church, which is His body, the fullness of Him who fills all in all" (Ephesians 1:22–23).

And Paul even told us why God established the Gentile churches on earth—to demonstrate something. Paul said, "To me, the very least of all saints, this grace was given, to preach to the Gentiles the unfathomable riches of Christ, and to bring to light what is the administration of the mystery which for ages has been hidden in God, who created all things; in order that the manifold wisdom of God might now be made known through the church to the rulers and the authorities in the heavenly places" (Ephesians 3:8–10).

I believe this demonstration of God's wisdom through the church has actually happened. Have you noticed? It seems the whole world is attempting to make itself into the American image. And, as I said before, I believe the true Christian church—represented in the Bible by the seven independent churches—is responsible for the freedoms and blessing achieved here in America and other free nations.

When the founding fathers of any nation see fit to make a place for these Bible-believing churches, they are actually providing a place for the kingdom of heaven to take root. And this kingdom of heaven has provided the world with a foretaste of the promised Messianic Kingdom that is to come (Mark 4:26–32, Romans 10:19–21).

But this age of the reign of the overcoming churches will come to an end. And when it does, that old satanic darkness will return. Beginning with Revelation 4, this is what we find occurring.

Whether the churches have been raptured at this point, or if they have lost their lampstands through a great falling away from the faith, is subject to debate.

But no matter what your view on this issue, in chapter 4 the churches have lost their lampstands, and the kingdom of heaven is no longer to be found holding back the satanic darkness anywhere on earth.

Remember, the book of Revelation was broken up into three parts. The first part was about the things John saw and the second part about the things which are—the overcoming churches. Now we've reached the third part—the things which take place after the things which are. This is why chapter 4, the beginning of the second part, starts out by saying, "After these things." In other words, starting with chapter 4, the events that occur are after the churches have lost their lampstands and the old satanic darkness has returned to reclaim its authority over the earth.

This new imbalance of power on earth calls for a response from heaven. So chapters 4 and 5 are about certain important events occurring in heaven. The first thing John describes to us are the thrones, and one of these thrones belongs to God. Then we read about a book that no one is worthy to open—no one, that is, except Jesus, the Lamb.

A parallel passage about these events that take place in heaven can be found in the book of Daniel (Daniel 7:9–10). When taken together, these prophecies seem to indicate that these events in heaven will occur after the Antichrist has been revealed to the world and is boasting great things.

When Jesus breaks the seals on the book, a terrible series of curses and plagues are unleashed on the Antichrist and his followers. Beginning with Revelation 6, we find the results of the breaking of the seven seals. After the seven seals, we have the sounding of the seven trumpets. And, after that, we have the pouring out on the earth of the seven bowls of God's wrath.

Believe me, you don't want to be around for this wrath stuff. Fortunately, God's wrath is not intended for His own people (1 Thessalonians 5:9). At some point in time before God's wrath is poured out on the Antichrist and his world, we will be out of here.

Whether already removed from earth by the rapture, or removed from earth through a great persecution, it won't matter. My point is that the wrath of God is not meant for His people. If you're one of His people, before God's wrath falls on earth, you will either be protected in some supernatural way, or you will be out of here. God's wrath is only for those who have rejected the grace of the Lord Jesus and have instead embraced the kingdom of the Antichrist.

At the end of these torments, the global economic and religious system known as Babylon will be destroyed in one hour with fire by the Antichrist. Then, as the nations of earth are gathered for war in the land of Israel, Jesus will suddenly appear in the clouds of heaven. And guess what? If you're a Christian today, you and I will be returning to the earth with Him. Believe it or not, we'll be taking our part in Christ's final victory over evil.

The Antichrist and the False Prophet will be cast into the Lake of Fire, and Satan will be bound and thrown into the Bottomless Pit. And then Jesus, and all of us who have returned with Him, will establish His long-awaited kingdom of righteousness. In other words, we win!

There is much more to this great book. But my intention is only to give you a quick overview. Now we'll move on to some of those difficult images of prophecy found in the book of Revelation.

Chapter 3 Notes

1. For a good study on this subject see chapter 4 of Tim Lahaye's book, *Revelation: Illustrated and Made Plain* (Grand Rapids: Zondervan Publishing House, 1975 Edition).

4

Using the Keys to Unlock the Signs

Now we're going to use those keys we learned in the second chapter to interpret some of the difficult images in the book of Revelation. Understanding the meaning of these images is important. When events in Europe and the Mediterranean begin to match the images in these prophecies, our world will begin witnessing the prophetic road signs leading to Christ's return. I believe this may be happening, and I will show why later in this book.

Sign 1: The Mother Of All Signs (Revelation 12:1–9)

The first image we need to understand is what might be called the mother of all signs. I say this because the Bible refers to this sign as a "great sign." In fact, if we don't understand this sign correctly, then we won't be able to understand all the signs in prophecy that follow.

Actually, this sign will be for the angels in heaven to see. We on earth, however, will come to appreciate its effects. When this sign is displayed an enormous battle for the heavenly high ground will erupt between God's angels and Satan and his angels. The Apostle John described the great sign like this: "And a great sign appeared in heaven: a woman clothed with the sun, and moon under her feet, and on her head a crown of twelve stars; and she was with child; and she cried out, being in labor and in pain to give birth" (Revelation 12:1–2).

Before we interpret this first great sign, we will examine another sign.

Sign 2: The Great Seven-Headed Dragon

Right after the first great sign comes another. John said:

> And another sign appeared in heaven and behold, a great dragon having seven heads and ten horns, and on his heads were seven diadems (crowns). And his tail swept away a third of the stars of heaven, and threw them to the earth. And the dragon stood before the woman who was about to give birth, so that when she gave birth he might devour her child (Revelation 12:3–4).

When I read about these two signs—the sign of the woman and the sign of the dragon—I envision two angelic armies quietly facing each other on a heavenly battlefield. Each side is waiting for the other to move first. Suddenly, the sign representing one side is raised high in the air and a loud cheer breaks out. Then another sign, representing the other side, appears and that army cheers.

But before the battle begins we find that the first sign about the woman wasn't finished yet. John describes the rest of the first sign:

> And she (the woman) gave birth to a son, a male child, who is to rule the nations with a rod of iron; and her child was caught up to God and to His throne. And the woman fled into the wilderness where she had a place prepared by God, so that there she might be nourished for one thousand two hundred and sixty days (3 1/2 years, Revelation 12:5–6).

Now the angelic battle begins. John wrote:

> And there was war in heaven, Michael and his angels waging war with the dragon. And the dragon and his angels waged war, and they were not strong enough, and there was no longer a place found for them in heaven. And the great dragon was thrown down, the serpent of old who is called the devil, and Satan, who deceives the whole world; he was thrown down to the earth, and his angels were thrown down with him (Revelation 12:7–9).

Who Is That Woman?

Who is the woman in this first sign? Since God called this "a great sign" it must be very important for us to get it right. Some believe this woman in labor represents the church. This is because a woman in Bible prophecy can represent religion. But how can the church—something that began after Jesus was born—give birth to Jesus (the child referred to in this passage)? Not only does this not make sense, but many Scripture passages point to a better interpretation.

As I've said, the correct identification of this woman is a very important issue. If your church claims that she is the same as the woman "clothed with the sun," I must give you a word of warning. There is another woman in Bible prophecy who also brings forth a messiah-like figure. But this is the "other woman." She represents false religion. But more on this later.

The simplest and best answer is that the woman in this great sign is Israel. And her child is the Messiah who was born from her and caught up into heaven. Of course, this child was Jesus.

So, once again, we find God mainly concerned about His purposes for Israel and the Messiah. Here, however, God expands His revelation by showing that there is a spiritual side to this earthly conflict. This seven-headed dragon represents Satan and the seven Gentile kingdoms he has used to oppose God's purposes for Israel.

We already know the identity of five of these kingdoms from King Nebuchadnezzar's dream. But the king's dream began in the time of Israel's captivity to Babylon, and this great sign covers a longer period of time. This image reveals this great earthly conflict from God's point of view, beginning with the time of His servant Abraham. According to H.L. Willmington, in his *Willmington's Guide to the Bible*, the seven Gentile kingdoms represented by the heads of this dragon are:

- Egypt, which enslaved Israel for 400 years (Exodus 1–12)
- Assyria, which captured the northern kingdom of Israel (2 Kings 17)
- Babylon, which captured the southern kingdom of Israel (2 Kings 24)
- Persia, which produced wicked Haman (Esther 3)
- Greece, which produced, indirectly, Antiochus Epiphanes (Daniel 11)
- Rome, which destroyed Jerusalem in A.D. 70 (see Luke 21) and which will torment Israel in the revived empire as never before in history (Revelation 12).[1]

In other words, the Roman Empire was the sixth head (kingdom). And a revived Roman Empire will be the seventh head (kingdom).

Once again, we must remember the on-going nature of these images. So, this woman in this great sign represents Israel, the nation God has chosen as His instrument to bring salvation to the world. And the dragon represents Satan and the seven major Gentile kingdoms he has used to oppose God's purposes for

Israel. So Satan is continually plotting to destroy the Messiah and His special nation, Israel.[2]

This interpretation is consistent with the keys. It's simple, and it matches the overlay of the king's statue.

The Bush That's Still Burning

As we've learned, an important key to unlocking our understanding of Bible prophecy is the nation of Israel. And, as we have just learned, Israel is the "great sign." It's important that we understand why. It's because God chose to work through the nation of Israel to reveal Himself to the world.

The Old Testament prophets were, above all, concerned with God's purposes for Israel and the surrounding nations. In fact, the Apostle Paul tells us that the existence of the Gentile church was not even revealed to the prophets of old (Ephesians 3:4–5). You see, the physical nation of Israel is God's on-going witness in the world to the reality of His existence. This is what God meant when he spoke to the nation of Israel through the prophet Isaiah:

> 'You are My witnesses,' declares the Lord, 'And My servant whom I have chosen, in order that you may know and believe Me, and understand that I am He. Before Me there was no God formed, and there will be none after Me. I, even I, am the Lord; and there is no savior besides Me' (Isaiah 43:10–11).

The role of Israel for God's purposes in history is symbolized in the burning bush. At that time, all of Israel was in slavery under the hard-hearted rule of Egypt's pharaoh. When the time came for God to deliver His people from bondage, God appeared to Moses in a bush that was on fire but was not being consumed.

Have you ever wondered why God appeared in this way? The bush represented the children of Israel and the fire represented God's anger. In other words, although Israel may experience His anger God would see to it that Israel would never be completely consumed (Isaiah 4:4, 5:25, 6:13, Zechariah 13:8–9).

When Moses asked God for His name, God answered, "I Am who I Am." This name that God gave to Moses was derived from the Hebrew verb, "to be." By using this name, God was emphasizing His eternal existence.

You see, not only was God planning to reveal His name and nature through the children of Israel, He was going to make their continuing existence a proof of His Own continuing existence. This is why—in the last book of the Old Testament—God reaffirmed His commitment to preserve His chosen people by promising through the prophet Malachi, "For I, the Lord, do not change: therefore you, O sons of Jacob, are not consumed" (Malachi 3:6).

Prophecy Stays Cool

But as a nation Israel did cease to exist. In A.D. 70, the Roman Emperor Titus completely destroyed God's favored city Jerusalem, and the Jewish people were scattered among the Gentile nations. Yet this too was predicted in Bible prophecy. Hundreds of years earlier Daniel wrote:

> Then after the sixty-two weeks the Messiah will be cut off and have nothing, and the people of the prince who is to come will destroy the city and the sanctuary. And its end will come with a flood; even to the end there will be war; desolations are determined (Daniel 9–26).

It is interesting to note that, at the time Daniel wrote these words, the temple in Jerusalem had already been destroyed by King Nebuchadnezzar's armies. This means it first had to be rebuilt, and then once again destroyed. And this is exactly what happened.

Yet even more interesting is the part about the Messiah first being cut off and having nothing. The only one this could have been referring to was Jesus. He's the only personality in history who could qualify as the Messiah that Daniel said would be "cut off and have nothing" before the destruction of Jerusalem in A.D. 70. Jesus was crucified less than forty years earlier.

Jesus also correctly predicted the destruction that was coming to Jerusalem. But when the destruction came in A.D. 70, not everything happened that Jesus said would happen. For example, Jesus said:

> Therefore when you see the abomination of desolation which was spoken of through Daniel the prophet, standing in the holy place, then let those who are in Judea flee to the mountains; let him who is on the housetop not go down to get the things out that are in his house; and let him who is in the field not turn back to get his cloak. But woe to those who are with child and to those who nurse babes in those days! But pray that your flight may not be in the winter or on the Sabbath; for then there will be a great tribulation, such as has not occurred since the beginning of the world until now, nor ever shall. And unless those days had been cut short, no life would have been saved; but for the sake of the elect those days shall be cut short (Matthew 24:15–22).

The Roman Legions devastated the little nation of Israel in A.D. 70. But as bad as it was, it was not the great tribulation Jesus spoke of—"a great tribulation, such as has not occurred since the beginning of the world until now, nor ever shall."

And Jesus certainly wasn't talking about that regional conflict fought with ancient weapons when He said, "unless those days had been cut short, no life would have been saved; but for the sake of the elect those days shall be cut short."

For students of Bible prophecy, the implications were clear. Although Israel had ceased to be a nation in A.D. 70, someday Israel would be reborn. And not only that, the temple would be rebuilt. Then the Antichrist and the Great Tribulation would come just as predicted by Daniel and Jesus.

One of these faithful students of prophecy was a man by the name of Clarence Larkin. His book, *Dispensational Truth* (1918), laid the groundwork for many of the students of Bible prophecy who followed him. What fascinates me about Clarence Larkin is how his absolute faith in Scripture foresaw the restoration of Israel many years before it happened. Like a child, he looked at the pictures in prophecy and believed them. And guess what? He was right.

A Miracle of the First Kind

The nation of Israel was reborn on May 14, 1948. It was a miracle of the first kind—a very "great sign." Never before has a nation ceased to exist for so long a time and then returned to become a nation again. And this is what the Jewish people were able to do after almost two thousand years in exile.

Yet this is what the prophecies said would happen. For example, the prophet Ezekiel said:

> The hand of the Lord was upon me, and He brought me out by the Spirit of the Lord and set me down in the middle of the valley; and it was full of bones. And He caused me to pass among them round about, and behold, there were very many on the surface of the valley; and lo, they were very dry. And He said to me, 'Son of man, can these bones live?' And I answered, 'O Lord God, Thou knowest.' Again He said to me, 'Prophecy over these *bones,* and say to them,' 'O dry bones, hear the word of the Lord. Thus says the Lord God to these bones, 'Behold, I will cause breath to enter you that you may come to life' (Ezekiel 37:1–5).

These dry bones represented "the whole house of Israel" (Ezekiel 37:11). And the question, "can these bones live," was asked by students of Bible prophecy for hundreds of years following Israel's destruction in A.D. 70. The Bible clearly taught that someday Israel was going to be reborn as a nation. Yet the fulfillment of this prophetic event seemed about as probable as life returning to a valley of dry bones.

So Ezekiel obeyed God and prophesied over the bones. And when he did, he saw the bones coming back to life. He said, "So I prophesied as He commanded me, and breath came into them, and they came to life, and stood on their feet, an exceedingly great army" (Ezekiel 37:1–10).

Then in 1948, the impossible happened. Just as Ezekiel prophesied, the dry bones began coming back to life. The nation of Israel was reborn. Even many unbelievers understood the prophetic implications of this event. One such person was the former Israeli Prime Minister, Benjamin Netanyahu. In a speech given in Washington to the American Jewish Community, Netanyahu said, "As you all know, I am not a religious man. But you don't have to be religious to see that the Jewish state is a fulfillment of prophecy."

Netanyahu then went on to list all the seemingly impossible events that happened to come together and give birth to his nation.

I remember a day when I was a small boy playing in my grandparent's front yard. My grandmother called me to the door and said something to me I will never forget. She said, "The Lord isn't coming in my lifetime, but He's coming in yours."

Then she turned away, closed the door, and left me standing alone with my thoughts. This happened in the early 1950s. During this time, I remember she would often sit in her chair and read her Bible. When she called me to the door she must have been reading the prophecies and thinking about the implications of the recent rebirth of Israel.

In my imagination, I can see her looking up and watching me play in her yard. Suddenly, the burden of God's Word in heart became too great to keep to herself. She had to tell someone. How do I know this is what happened? Because many times now I have felt the very same way.

It's very possible that my grandmother's prediction—that I would be alive when Christ returns—might come true. This is because she had strong biblical support for her view. Jesus said that when the nation of Israel was reborn and certain signs began to occur then that generation of the Jewish race would live to see the end times. He put it this way:

> Now learn the parable from the fig tree; when its branch has already become tender, and puts forth its leaves, you know that summer is near; even so you

too, when you see all these things, recognize that He is near, right at the door. Truly I say to you, this generation will not pass away until all these things take place (Matthew 24:32–34).

This fig tree is Israel. God often referred to Israel in such fashion. Speaking through Hosea, God said, "I found Israel like grapes in the wilderness; I saw your forefathers as the earliest fruit on the fig tree in its first season" (Hosea 9:10). In another place God said, "Thus says the Lord God of Israel, 'Like these good figs, so I will regard as good the captives of Judah, whom I have sent out of this place into the land of the Chaldeans" (Jeremiah 23:5).

Jesus' comparison of Israel to a fig tree may explain a confusing passage in the New Testament—when Jesus cursed the fig tree. Once, when Jesus became hungry, He walked up to a fig tree in order to eat some of its fruit. Although the tree was in full leaf, there was no fruit on it. So Jesus said to the tree, "May no one ever eat fruit from you again."

Later when Jesus and His disciples passed by this tree again, Peter noticed that the fig tree had withered from its roots up. When Peter asked about this, Jesus responded by saying: "Have faith in God. Truly I say to you, whoever says to this mountain. 'Be taken up and cast into the sea,' and does not doubt in his heart, but believes that what he says is going to happen, it shall be granted him" (Mark11:23).

Like that fig tree, we can have leaves—we can appear very religious. But, if we don't have our faith rooted deep in Jesus, then we won't have power to bear any real fruit for God. In fact, this is what happened to Israel when they rejected Jesus as their Messiah.

So, when Jesus asks us to "learn the parable from the fig tree," He was telling us not to make the same mistake as unbelieving Israel. And when He said, "this generation will not pass away until all these things take place," He was referring to the generation that sees the rebirth of Israel and the beginning of the signs—our generation.

So, when Israel was reborn on that day in 1948, our world witnessed the first sign of the end-times events in the book of Revelation. This first sign was the sudden reappearance of the nation of Israel on the world stage.

And we know that when this first "great sign" of the woman appears, another sign is soon to follow. And that second sign—which I believe began with the Schuman Declaration in 1950—is the appearance of the great seven-headed dragon.

Sign 3: The B...B...B...Beast! (Revelation 13:1–2)

Now we get to the spooky part. The beast of Revelation makes his grand entrance. John wrote:

> And he (the dragon—Satan) stood on the sand of the sea shore. And I saw a beast coming up out of the sea having ten horns and seven heads, and on his horns were ten diadems (crowns), and on his heads were blasphemous names. And the beast which I saw was like a leopard, and his feet were like those of a bear, and his mouth like the mouth of a lion. And the dragon gave him his power and his throne and great authority (Revelation 13:1–2).

Once again—to identify this beast—we need to use those keys. We have learned from Key 6 to look at things from God's point of view. And from God's point of view a beast is an evil king and his kingdom.

But what king and kingdom could this be? This is where we can use that image of the statue King Nebuchadnezzar saw as an overlay. Remember, the statue represented the four great Gentile empires that would rise over Israel until the Messiah came. The fourth and last kingdom was Rome. This could only mean that the beast John saw rising from the sea in Revelation is some kind of revival of the Roman Empire.

This dream of the statue, however, was from a pagan king's point of view. If you recall, we also have another picture of this last Gentile empire from God's point of view given to Daniel. Let's see if the beast Daniel saw representing Rome fits the description of this beast John saw in Revelation. Daniel wrote:

> After this I kept looking in the night visions, and behold, a fourth beast, dreadful and terrifying and extremely strong; and it had large iron teeth. It devoured and crushed, and trampled down the remainder with its feet; and it was different from all the beasts that were before it, and it had ten horns (Daniel 7:7).

Bingo! The beast Daniel saw had 10 horns. And the beast John saw in Revelation also had ten horns. So this 10-horned beast John saw rising from the sea must be some kind of replay of the old Roman Empire.

Yet the beast not only had 10 horns, it also had seven heads. And one of these heads had a fatal wound. John said, "And I saw one of his heads as if it had been slain, and his fatal wound was healed. And the whole earth was amazed and followed after the beast" (Revelation 13:3).

There has been much speculation about the meaning of this head wound. A popular interpretation today is that the Antichrist will be killed and come back to life. People who hold this view believe that this coming back to life would be an attempt by Satan to duplicate Christ's death and resurrection.

So will the Antichrist rise from the dead? If you have seen the movie, *The Omega Code*, this is probably what you're expecting to happen. The movie presents a fictionalized story based on many of today's popular interpretations of Bible prophecy. The movie was well made, and I enjoyed it very much. The most powerful scene is when the Antichrist, portrayed by the great actor Michael York, awakens from the dead after receiving a fatal gunshot wound to the head.

But is this an accurate interpretation of prophecy? I have several problems with this idea. For one thing, this interpretation is based entirely on speculation. But even more importantly, it's an unnecessary speculation.

One of our keys to the prophecies in Revelation is to understand what came before. In the book of Genesis, this great red dragon is depicted as a small serpent that successfully tempts our first human ancestors to join him in his rebellion against God. Because of this evil deed, God told the serpent: "And I will put enmity between you and the woman, and between your seed and her seed; He shall bruise (crush) you on the head, and you shall bruise him on the heel" (Genesis 3:15).

Here we find the beginning of a conflict between good and evil that is destined to span the farthest reaches of human development and history. In Genesis, we see God beginning a process for delivering His people from the effects of their fall into sin and the power of the serpent. This Savior would be the promised seed of the woman who would someday crush the serpent's head.

Of course, we Christians know that this Savior has already come and given that serpent of old his fatal blow. This occurred when Jesus died on the cross. Referring to His coming death and resurrection, Jesus said, "Now judgment is upon the world; now the ruler of this world shall be cast out. And I, if I be lifted up from the earth, will draw all men to Myself" (John 12:31–32).

You see, when Christ was crucified, Satan and his Roman Empire—the sixth head of the great red dragon—received their fatal head wound. This is why Jesus said after His resurrection, "All authority has been given to Me in heaven and earth" (Matthew 28:18).

But someday, perhaps sooner than we think, the Roman Empire, with Satan himself ruling over it in the form of the Antichrist, will return (Revelation 13:1–3). And, as John said, the whole earth will be amazed.

10 Horns of a Dilemma

Now we need to know what the 10 horns on this beast of Revelation represent. But this is no problem. The Bible provides us with the answer in Revelation. These 10 horns are 10 kings who will rule with the Antichrist (Revelation 17:12).

Again, this is consistent with Daniel's vision of the beast that represented Rome. Daniel described this fourth beast by saying:

> While I was contemplating the horns, behold another horn, a little one came up among them, and three of the first horns were pulled out by the roots before it; and behold the horn possessed eyes like the eyes of a man, and a mouth uttering great boasts (Daniel 7:8).

As we know, a beast in Bible prophecy doesn't only represent a kingdom, it also represents some great king. In the case of this terrible beast of Revelation, that king will be the Antichrist himself. In other words, the Roman Empire will someday return in the form of 10 kings, and the Antichrist will rise to power among them.

Many excellent Bible scholars share this understanding of prophecy. One such scholar is John Walvoord. In his book, *The Nations in Prophecy*, Walvoord says:

> A crisis in the Mediterranean area leads to the formation of the revived Roman Empire composed of a ten-nation confederacy. This is occasioned by the rise of the Roman 'prince that shall come' (Daniel 9:26) who subdues three of the kings and secures the submission of the seven remaining rulers. His successful conquest of these ten kingdoms, outlined in Daniel 7:23–26, makes the Roman ruler supreme in his control of this revived form of the ancient Roman Empire.[3]

Sign 4: The Antichrist's Sidekick (Revelation 13:11–14)

As if this first beast from the sea wasn't enough bad news, John tells us that another beast comes up. But this one's from the earth. John wrote:

> And I saw another beast coming up out of the earth; and he had two horns like a lamb, and he spoke as a dragon. And he exercises all the authority of the first beast in his presence. And he makes the earth and those who dwell in it to worship the first beast, whose fatal wound was healed. And he performed great

signs, so that he even makes fire come down out of heaven to the earth in the presence of men (Revelation 13:11–13).

This two-horned beast is usually referred to as the "False Prophet" (Revelation19:20). This creepy creature will bring fire down from heaven and cause people to worship the Antichrist. But there is more to this guy.

Remember, these beasts of Bible prophecy aren't only kings. They are also kingdoms that have some kind of relationship to Israel. And when we read a little farther, we find that this beast has more than just spiritual authority. About this second beast John writes:

> And he causes all, the small and the great, and the rich and the poor, and the free men and the slaves, to be given a mark on their right hand, or on their forehead, and he provides that no one should be able to buy or to sell, except the one who has the mark, either the name of the beast or the number of his name (Revelation 13:16–17).

Here we have one man who has immense religious and economic power. In fact, I believe this could be the meaning of his two horns. "Horns" in Bible prophecy indicate power. This man's power will be religious and economic.

This suggests that this person will have control over some kind of global organization where he can exercise these two powers. Where would we look to find such an organization today? I believe this organization could well be the United Nations. Later in the book, I will deal more with why I believe the United Nations could be the organization destined to fall under the control of the False Prophet.

If I'm right, and the first beast (the Antichrist and his kingdom) is now rising from the sea, then it won't be long until the second beast (the False Prophet and his kingdom) also shows up.

Sign 5: The Other Woman

Remember the other woman I mentioned a while back? Well the time has come to introduce you to that other woman—the scarlet lady of prophecy. John wrote:

> And one of the seven angels who had the seven bowls came and spoke with me, saying, 'Come here, I shall show you the judgment of the great harlot who sits on many waters with whom the kings of the earth committed acts of immorality, and those who dwell on the earth were made drunk with the wine of her

immorality.' And he carried me away in the Spirit into a wilderness; and I saw a woman sitting on a scarlet beast, full of blasphemous names, having seven heads and ten horns. And the woman was clothed in purple and scarlet, and adorned with gold and precious stones and pearls, having in her hand a gold cup full of abominations and of the unclean things of her immorality, and upon her forehead a name was written, a mystery, 'BABYLON THE GREAT, THE MOTHER OF HARLOTS AND OF THE ABOMINATIONS OF THE EARTH.' And I saw the woman drunk with the blood of the saints, and with the blood of the witnesses of Jesus. And I wondered greatly (Revelation 17:1–6). I don't know about you, but this is one of those places where I can really relate to the Apostle John. Every time I've read his description of this woman riding the beast, I too have "wondered greatly."

Yet the next thing the angel said to John was, "Why do you wonder? I shall tell you the mystery of the woman and the beast that carries her, which has seven heads and the ten horns."

Talk about someone being frustrated! What the angel said to help us understand the meaning of the woman riding the beast seems even harder to understand. But more on that later.

I agree with the commonly accepted view of this passage. The woman riding the beast represents false religion. As we have learned, these images of Bible prophecy are from God's point of view. So this false religion is the one that—from God's point of view—gave birth to all false religions. That's why she's called "THE MOTHER OF HARLOTS."

Like the other images in prophecy, this image has an on-going nature. That is the reason she is called, "BABYLON THE GREAT." This identifies this false religion with the ancient Babylonian Empire. Tim Lahaye said, "In ancient days Satan seemed to make Babylon the capital of his evil operation. From this headquarters was started false religion" (*Revelation Illustrated and Made Plain* p. 224).

But Alexander Hislop, author of the great Christian classic *The Two Babylons*, traced the false religion in ancient Babylon back to the builders of the Tower of Babel.[4] According to the Bible, the Tower of Babel is where people who had rebelled against God came together to build a city. These people said, "Come, let us build for ourselves a city, and a tower whose top will reach into heaven, and let us make for ourselves a name; lest we be scattered abroad over the face of the whole earth" (Genesis 11:4).

Hislop believes the religion that began at the Tower of Babel was actually the worship of Satan in the form of fire, the sun and the serpent.[5] However, Satan worship could not be done openly because of the many who still believed in the true God of Noah. So a mystery religion began at Babel where Satan could be worshipped in secret.

These builders of Babel had a leader by the name of Nimrod. The Bible tells us that Nimrod "became a mighty one on the earth." In fact, the city of Babel was just the beginning of Nimrod's great empire. He went on to build and unite seven more great cites (Genesis 10:8–12).

There is non-biblical support for the existence of this great leader. According to ancient lore, Nimrod had a wife named Semiramis. Although Nimrod recognized no God other than himself, Semiramis was religious. And she was the one responsible for the creation of the idolatrous mystery religion that began at Babel.

So at Babel, we find the first rebellious builders of a godless system of government and the first promoters of this idolatrous mystery religion. These two forces worked together to blind and enslave the weak and spiritually ignorant people in the days of Nimrod.

Of course we know the rest of the story. God interrupted the plans of these builders by giving them different languages. Unfortunately, as these people scattered, they carried their mystery religion with them over the face of the whole earth.

So the woman John saw riding the beast represents this satanically inspired religion that has been scattered around the world, now existing in its many forms.

A Beast Only Its Mother Could Love

This brings us back to the beast John saw this mystery woman riding. The angel said:

> The beast that you saw was and is not, and is about to come up out of the abyss and to go to destruction. And those who dwell on the earth will wonder, whose name has not been written in the book of life from the foundation of the world, when they see the beast, that he was and is not and will come (Revelation 17:18).

What in the world does this beast stand for? Perhaps the simplest explanation is that the beast that "was" refers to Satan when he appeared to Eve in the form of a serpent in the Garden of Eden.

If so, then the beast that "is not" refers to the fact that Satan, at the time of John, didn't occupy an earthly body. And the beast that "is about to come up out of the abyss" means that someday Satan will occupy another earthly body, but this next time it will be the body of a human king. If you follow this interpretation, then you can see why some Christians believe that Satan himself will someday personally indwell the Antichrist.

Yet I don't agree with this interpretation. For one thing, Revelation 16:13 indicates that they remain separate beings. In this passage we find the dragon (representing Satan) and the beast (representing the Antichrist) still being referred to separately.

Another problem with the interpretation that Satan personally indwells the Antichrist is that the "abyss"—the place where the beast comes out from—is another name for the "bottomless pit." And Satan does not dwell in the bottomless pit. This is where demons dwell. Demons are spirits that do not have their own bodies.

According to Clarence Larkin, the abyss is "the prison house of demons (Revelation 9:1–21), and where Satan is to be bound for 1000 years (Revelation 20:1–3, 7–8)." Larkin said, "It is the place into which the demons besought Christ not to send them" (Luke 8:31). Then Larkin summed it up by saying:

The 'Bottomless Pit' or 'Abyss' then is a deeper compartment in 'The Underworld' than 'Paradise,' or 'Hell,' and is the place where the 'demons' and baser spirits are temporarily confined until they are finally consigned to the 'Lake of Fire' to spend eternity with their Master, Satan.[6] So if it isn't Satan, then who—or what—is this beast that the angel said would "come up out of the abyss and go to destruction?"

According to Larkin, "the 'King' of the 'Bottomless Pit' is called in the Hebrew tongue 'Abaddon,' but in the Greek tongue his name is 'Apollyon,' that is, the King of the 'Bottomless Pit' is named after the Hebrew and Greek words that are translated—'Destruction.'"

Here we may have some important clues to identifying this beast. We know for sure that this beast from the abyss refers to the coming Antichrist. We also have learned that the name of the king of the abyss—the place the beast comes out of—is "Destruction." And we also know that Paul called the Antichrist "the son of destruction" (2 Thessalonians 2:3).

This is why I believe the beast from the abyss refers to some demon spirit who is specifically used by Satan to possess certain earthly kings. And when this possession occurs, it's as if Satan himself were the king.

When Satan appeared to Eve in the Garden of Eden, it was in a time of innocence. It was before Adam and Eve ate the fruit—before the fall of mankind had occurred. At that time, Satan and his demons didn't have the right to occupy a human being. This is why Satan first had to appear in the body of a serpent. Since the fall, however, human bodies have become available.

Now when people worship Satan instead of God, whether knowingly or not, Satan and his demons can gain the right to occupy their bodies. This is Satan's true purpose for false religion.

So, let's put this all together. This woman John saw riding the beast represents this satanically inspired religion scattered around the world. This false religion likes to work together with godless governments. And the beast represents Satan's ultimate goal of bringing his Antichrist demon from the abyss to indwell some powerful earthly king. When this occurs, this king becomes Satan in the flesh. And these two forces working together are called by the Apostle Paul, "the mystery of lawlessness" (2 Thessalonians 2:7).

If you have come to a different interpretation of these verses that's OK. These are difficult passages to understand and I don't for one minute think I have found all the right answers.

Those Heads are Mountains and Kings

The angel went on to explain a little more about the beast the woman of false religion was sitting on. The angel said:

> Here is the mind which has wisdom. The seven heads are seven mountains on which the woman sits, and they are seven kings; five have fallen, one is, the other has not yet come; and when he comes he must remain a little while. And the beast which was and is not, is himself also an eighth, and is one of the seven, and he goes to destruction (Revelation 17:9–11).

Some Bible versions use the word "hills" in place of "mountains," which the New American Standard version uses. And since the city of Rome is known to sit on seven hills, this causes some prophecy students to identify this woman riding the beast with the Vatican and the Catholic Church.

And this leads some to believe that the seven kings this passage refers to were seven Roman Emperors. The problem with this interpretation is that these seven emperors are hard to specifically identify. And if you recall from our keys, we are to watch for sure road signs in history, not unidentifiable events or emperors.

It's my opinion that this is another example of a dual prophecy. At the time this was written, it was clearly understood that this prophecy referred to the city of Rome. In fact, in John's day, Roman coins were even circulating with the seven hills of Rome on their face. And, as you know, John and the early Christians went through much persecution because of this woman riding the beast—because of opposing false religion and Roman authority.

However, it doesn't necessarily follow that the end-times fulfillment will also refer to the literal city of Rome. Let me show you why.

For one thing, I can't see the Antichrist making Rome—one of his own capital cities—a great wasteland in one hour with fire, such as the Antichrist is predicted to do to this harlot at the end of the tribulation (Revelation 17:16–18).

For another, most Bible translators believe the correct word is "mountains," not "hills."[7] But my main reason for believing the correct word is "mountains" is because this would make this prophecy more consistent with those prophecies that have come before.

The angel's statement that the seven heads of the beast are mountains and kings may at first seem more confusing. Actually it is very helpful to our understanding. If you recall, the future kingdom of the Messiah was pictured in King Nebuchadnezzar's dream as a great mountain (Daniel 2:35). Other Old Testament prophets also referred to great kings and their kingdoms who opposed Israel as mountains (Isaiah 2:2, Zechariah 4:7).

At the time of John, five of these great kingdoms that the woman sat on had come and gone. These were Egypt, Assyria, Babylon, Medo-Persia and Greece. The one that existed in John's day was Rome.

Now the angel's attention turns from the earthly kings of these kingdoms back to the beast that comes from the pit. The angel says, "And the beast which was and is not, is himself also an eighth, and is one of the seven, and he goes to destruction."

In other words, at the time John wrote these words, the beast was back in the Bottomless Pit. But someday, when the Roman Empire is revived under a confederacy of 10 nations, a seventh king will come to power.

And after this seventh king comes to power, the beast will again come out of the pit and possess this seventh king. When this event occurs, the beast from the pit will become the eighth king, and also will be one of the seven.

Again, there are other ways to interpret these difficult passages of prophecy. But as I consider all of our keys, this seems to be the best.

Slip, Sliding Away

If you recall, I said that this other woman of prophecy—the one who represents false religion—will also bring forth a messiah-like figure into the world. Before the true Messiah returns from heaven, a false messiah will be offered to the world. Unlike the Messiah who fulfilled the prophecies of Scripture—who came forth from Israel, died and rose again—this false messiah will come forth from false religion and use deceiving signs and wonders (2 Thessalonians 2:9).

The Apostle Paul explained it this way, "Let no one in any way deceive you, for it (Christ's return) will not come unless the apostasy comes first, and the man of lawlessness is revealed, the son of destruction" (2 Thessalonians 2:3).

The word "apostasy" means to fall away. Paul is telling us that, just before the Lord's return, most people will fall away from the true faith of the Bible.

When you think about it, it's amazing how confident the Apostle Paul was in the power of the new faith he was spreading. At the time Paul wrote this, the Christian faith had just begun to be preached. Yet here Paul was saying that the day would come when the loss of the true Christian faith would cause a calamitous political change to the entire world.

How could Paul, 2000 years ago, have had such confidence in the faith he was preaching? I believe it was because he understood the implications of what Jesus accomplished on the cross. Paul took it literally when Jesus said, "Now judgment is upon this world; now the ruler of this world shall be cast out. And I, if I be lifted up from the earth, will draw all men to Myself" (John 12:31–32).

Paul understood that our real battle here on earth is not against "flesh and blood," but against "the spiritual forces of wickedness" (Ephesians 6:12). He also knew that when Jesus was crucified, Satan's authority over mankind had finally been broken. Just as foretold in Bible prophecy, the seed of the woman had come (Jesus), and had crushed the serpent's (Satan's) head (Genesis 3:15).

You see, with true Christianity comes true freedom. And Paul knew that Christianity would have a liberating effect on the Gentile world that had been enslaved by Satan. As I said earlier in my book, I believe this is what Paul had in mind when he said:

> To me, the very least of the saints, this grace was given, to preach to the Gentiles the unfathomable riches of Christ…in order that the manifold wisdom of God might now be made known through the church to the rulers and the authorities in the heavenly places (Ephesians 3:8–10).

Now world leaders are attempting to mold their nations and international organizations into the American image—democracy, the rule of law, and individual freedom. Ironically, these world leaders can recognize the good that has been manifested by the nations that are filled with Bible-believing churches, but they can't bring themselves to recognize the faith that accomplished this good.

Yet after 2,000 years, how can we know for sure the true faith that Jesus started? Actually, this is an easy question to answer. Paul said:

> Now I make known to you, brethren, the gospel which I preached to you, which also you received, in which also you stand, by which also you are saved, if you hold fast the word which I preached to you, unless you believed in vain. For I delivered to you as of first importance what I also received, that Christ died for our sins according to the Scriptures, and that He was buried, and that He was raised on the third day according to the Scriptures" (1 Corinthians 15:1–4).

In other words, the Gospel message at the heart of the Christian faith is simple. If you truly believe in the death, burial and resurrection of Jesus, then you are a Christian. Yet, though the Gospel is very simple, it's also extremely powerful. Paul said, "For I am not ashamed of the gospel, for it is the power of God for salvation to everyone who believes" (Romans 1:16).

This is why our falling away from this wonderful Gospel is so strange. There is no natural reason for this to happen. The Bible tells us we will fall away from this simple Gospel because we will be seduced by that other woman of prophecy, false religion.

Paul wrote Timothy, "But the Spirit explicitly says that in the later times some will fall away from the faith (the simple gospel message), paying attention to deceitful spirits and doctrines of demons" (1 Timothy 4:1).

There is a reason the Spirit warned so explicitly about this falling away. When it happens on a large enough scale, the liberating influence Christianity brought into the Gentile world by Jesus will be taken out of Satan's way. I believe this is what Paul was referring to when he said, "For the mystery of lawlessness is already at work; only he who now restrains will do so until he is taken out of the way" (2 Thessalonians 2:7).

Sign 6: That Scary Number 666

There is one more sign in prophecy we need to take a look at. At the end of chapter 13, where John describes the 10-horned beast he saw rising from the sea, he throws a weird number at us.

John wrote, "Here is wisdom. Let him who has understanding calculate the number of the beast, for the number is that of a man; and his number is six hundred and sixty-six" (Revelation 13:18).

For 2,000 years, Christians have wondered about the meaning of that number. This has given rise to all kinds of speculation. Since the Hebrew and Greek alphabets use letters for numbers, there have been many attempts to match certain names to this number.

The occult world has also made use of this mysterious number. Constance Cumbey, an expert on the New Age movement, told me that some people who are involved in the New Age movement believe the number 666 brings them occultic power. They believe the more times they can use this number in their documents and logos, the more power will be granted to them.

As I thought about the occultic use of the number 666, I realized that Satan has gone to a great effort to hide the true meaning of this prophetic sign. God has not placed anything in the Bible that doesn't have a good purpose for God's people. From God's point of view there is nothing mystical about the number 666. It's just another prophetic sign God wants His people to watch for. John had more to say about this number. He wrote:

> And he (the False Prophet) causes all, the small and the great, and the rich and the poor, and the free men and the slaves, to be given a mark on their right hand, or on their forehead, and he provides that no one should be able to buy or sell, except the one who has the mark, either the name of the beast or the number of his name (Revelation 13:16–17).

In his book, *Dispensational Truth*, Clarence Larkin observed:

> The number '666' is the 'number of man,' and stops short of the perfect number seven. Man was created on the sixth day. Goliath the opposer of God's people, a type of Satan, was 6 cubits in height, he had 6 pieces of armor, and his spearhead weighed 600 shekels. Nebuchadnezzar's Image, a type of the 'Image of the Beast,' was 60 cubits in height, 6 cubits wide, and 6 instruments of music summoned the worshippers. [8]

Some Bible students have speculated that this "mark" will be some kind of computer chip with that number implanted under people's skin. Without this implanted chip, no one will be able to buy or sell. With e-commerce growing today by leaps and bounds, it's not hard to believe this may soon be possible—if not already.But this is all speculation. As I've already said, I believe Satan has gone to great effort to hide from the world the true meaning of this number found in Bible prophecy. Yet this can also be said about all the other prophetic signs in the Bible. Satan simply does not want us to understand any of them.

We have already learned that these Bible prophecies have mainly to do with real historical facts about Israel. I believe the number 666 is no different. It simply will identify a very evil man who, in the last days, will do terrible violence to Israel and God's people. In so doing, this man will bring great destruction from God upon himself and the whole earth.

And, believe it or not, in Europe today there is an important man who may hold a key to great political and military power, and that key is identified with the number 666.

Stay tuned.

Chapter 4 Notes

1. H. L. Willmington, *Willmington's Guide to the Bible* (Wheaton: Tyndale House Publishers, Inc., 1981) 565.

2. J. Dwight Pentecost, *Things to Come*, 285–90.

3. John F. Walvoord, *The Nations in Prophecy*, 103.

4. Alexander Hislop, *The Two Babylons*, 2nd American ed. (Neptune, New Jersey: Loizeaux Brothers, 1959) 5, 24.

5. Ibid., 227.

6. Clarence Larkin, *The Spirit World* (Glenside, Pennsylvania: 1921) 50.

7. Alfred Marshall, trans., *The Interlinear Greek-English New Testament* (Grand Rapids: Zondervan Publishing House, 1975), 761.; Joseph H. Thayer, trans., *Thayer's Greek-English Lexicon of the New Testament*, 4th ed. (Grand Rapids: Baker Book House, 1977) 454.

8. Clarence Larkin, *Dispensational Truth* (Philadelphia: Rev. Clarence Larkin Estate, 1920)124–5.

PART II

5

Apocalypse Now?

o o o o o o o o o o o o o o o o o o o o o o o o o o o o o o o o o

Some of our readers, looking at Europe as it now exists, may find it difficult to believe that it will ever be found gathered together into one empire. But when God interferes directly with the affairs of the world, He will carry out quickly what He has long since foretold will be the course of events.[1]

—*Alfred H. Burton, 1915*

Bible prophecy gives us signs of the end times. Just like road signs, they come closer together as we near the end. According to the Bible, in the last days—in a time when Israel has been restored as a nation (the first great sign)—a 10-nation confederacy will appear on the European continent. It will be a revival of the Roman Empire. From this confederacy, one man will rise to power. He will make a seven-year security agreement with Israel, which he will break in three and a half years. This man is known as the Antichrist and, in some way, he will be identified with the number 666.

Are You Sitting Down?

Now we are getting to the heart of my book. What if I said that an important warning sign about the rise of the Antichrist began occurring in 1992, but it has been completely overlooked? And what if I told you that the 10 kings of Daniel and Revelation may have already been on scene since 1995, but no one has noticed? Not only that, but a powerful new office has been created that could soon be occupied by the Antichrist.

On top of all of this, what would you say if I told you that the man who currently holds this office was recently given emergency powers with these 10 kings, and the document the EU leaders were acting on when they gave him these powers was titled "Assembly Recommendation 666?" Hang on, because that's exactly what I'm about to tell you.

Numbers Count

It's amazing how many times God answered my prayer, and I didn't notice until a long time later. I'd been writing a weekly religion column for quite some time before I realized that the column was a direct answer to a prayer.

It was a prayer motivated by a challenge. Jesus said, "If you abide in Me, and My words abide in you, ask what ever you wish, and it shall be done for you. By this is My father glorified, that you bear much fruit, and so prove to be My disciples" (John 15:7–8).

When I read this I realized that Jesus is interested in numbers. In fact, He's so interested in us winning souls for Christ that He challenges us to ask Him for anything we need to achieve that goal. He says this is the way to glorify the Father and prove that we are His disciples.

So I asked God to provide me with a way to reach more people. Soon I was writing a religion column that was appearing in up to five newspapers every week. This is a reason I believe God may have had His hand on the making of this book from the very beginning.

Over the past 10 years, I've written many columns. As I look through them, details from the past come back as if they were from yesterday. I began writing my columns about the time of the Gulf War. Since I was hopelessly interested in Bible prophecy, anything about the Middle East or Europe caught my attention.

I Saw the News Today…Oh Boy

o o o o o o o o o o o o o o o o o o o o o o o o o o o o o o o o o o o

…we can expect that one of tomorrow's headlines will announce the formation of a confederation of ten nations in the general area of the old Roman Empire—western Europe.[2]

—Charles C. Ryrie, 1969

One day I saw a report in the *Los Angeles Times* about a European military alliance known as the Western European Union (WEU). What caught my attention was the map showing the 10 European nations that belonged to this alliance. I immediately recalled the Bible prophecies about the revival of the Roman Empire under 10 kings. At that moment, the pastor of my church walked into my office. Since he was also interested in prophecy, I showed him the map.

"Doesn't this look a little like the old Roman Empire?" I asked.

"It is the old Roman Empire," he said.

This is how my long interest in a military alliance known as the Western European Union began. It turned out that, at that time, this military alliance was only nine nations: Belgium, France, Germany, Italy, Luxembourg, Netherlands, Portugal, Spain and the United Kingdom.

This confused me at first. Then I found that the reason the *Los Angeles Times* reported it as 10 nations was because Greece was scheduled to enter later in January of 1995. Another aspect about this alliance that tended to hide its possible prophetic significance was the fact that it was actually made up of 28 European nations. At that time, the 28 nations in the WEU were divided into four different types of membership. There were 10 Member States, three Associate Members, five Observers and 10 Associate Partners. Only the 10 Member States, however, had full voting rights.

In other words, only 10 nations were actually in control of the WEU military alliance. These, indeed, could become the 10 kings of Bible prophecy. I decided to take a closer look at the Western European Union.

Even 10-Horned Beasts Have Birthdays

o o o o o o o o o o o o o o o o o o o o o o o o o o o o o
During the wars preceding the rise of Antichrist the nations that will then be found in the geographical limits of the Old Roman Empire will form an 'Alliance' for mutual protection. Those nations will be ten in number, represented by the 'Ten Horns' of the Beast.[3]

—Clarence Larkin, 1920

It happened just like Clarence Larkin said. The Western European Union was born October 23, 1954. But it grew out of a five-nation mutual defense alliance that was founded at the end of World War II. These five European nations were concerned that they needed to protect themselves against a possible threat from the powerful Soviet Union. So on March 17, 1948, these nations signed the

Brussels Treaty. Article Four under this treaty bound them together in a mutual defense agreement, meaning that an attack against one would be an attack against all. These nations were Belgium, France, Luxembourg, the Netherlands and the United Kingdom.

But, after a short time, this defense agreement became inactive. When America, Canada and a few other European countries saw the resolve of these Brussels Treaty nations, they decided to contribute to the security of Europe. This led to the creation of the military alliance we now know as NATO on April 4, 1949, with the signing of the North Atlantic Treaty.

At this time, the responsibility these five European nations had to each other for mutual defense was transferred to NATO. Their non-military obligations under the Brussels Treaty, however, continued.

Then it happened. The military alliance known as the Western European Union was born on October 23, 1954, when the Brussels Treaty was modified to allow the entrance of Germany and Italy. Their collective defense agreement under Article Four in the old treaty was now under Article Five of the modified Brussels Treaty.

Yet even under the expanded provisions of the modified Brussels Treaty, the new WEU military alliance was born dead. I say this because, when all was said and done, the American-dominated NATO was still the alliance in charge of the defense of Europe. Like it or not, the Brussels Treaty nations realized they needed a big brother, like America, to defend themselves against the powerful Soviet Union. Yet they didn't like having to depend on America. So—although committed to the NATO alliance—these European nations went ahead with their original plans in the Brussels Treaty. They created their own military alliance in the WEU, looking forward to the day when they could go it alone. And when the Cold War was over and the Soviet threat was no more, that day would come.

Later, Portugal, Spain and Greece would also be allowed to join Europe's exclusive, new military club, the WEU. Together, these 10 nations became known as the Brussels Treaty Powers. And it was this inner circle of 10 European nations that controlled the WEU.

When the Brussels Treaty Powers that controlled the WEU reached 10, in January 1995, they had reached the magic number that students of Bible prophecy had been waiting for. Now all I could do was wait and see what would happen next.

Give the 10-Horned Kid a Chance

o o o o o o o o o o o o o o o o o o o o o o o o o o o o o o o

For the mystery of lawlessness is already at work; only he who now restrains will do so until he is taken out of the way.[4]

—*Apostle Paul, A.D. 50*

I realized that the beast of Revelation and the WEU had a lot in common, making me start to wonder if they were one and the same. They both had 10 horns, and they both wanted to take their place on the world stage. But something was holding them back.

Yet this is what the Bible tells us. It says the evil spiritual forces trying to raise this beast from the sea—the beast being the revived Roman Empire and the Antichrist—are already at work. Fortunately, God has been holding these evil spiritual forces back.

This is what the Apostle Paul meant when he said:

> For the mystery of lawlessness is already at work, only he who now restrains will do so until he is taken out of the way. And then that lawless one will be revealed whom the Lord will slay with the breath of His mouth and bring to an end by the appearance of His coming (2 Thessalonians 2:7–8).

The mystery of lawlessness has a religious side to it. Satan wishes to destroy the true faith found in the Bible. You see, the Gospel of Jesus Christ has been interfering with Satan's grip on the world since the time of the Roman Empire.

Where true Christianity has been accepted in the world, Satan's mystery of lawlessness has been restrained. And when this faith we find preserved in the Bible has been lost, Satan's mystery of lawlessness has returned. This is what the Apostle John meant by saying, "greater is He who is in you than he who is in the world" (1 John 4:4).

My point is, God used America—a nation known for its many Bible-believing churches—to liberate Europe from the tyranny of Hitler. And after the war, God again used America to establish the NATO alliance that has proven so successful in holding back atheistic Communism and keeping the peace in Europe.

If the 10 Brussels Treaty Powers in the WEU are to become the 10 kings of Bible prophecy that the Antichrist will rise from, then God has been using America to restrain the rise of the 10-horned beast of Revelation. This being the case, it won't require the rapture of the church for America to lose her restraining power in the world. All that would be required is for the churches in America to fall away from the faith and the authority of the Bible.

And if this falling away should happen, then the consequence may well be the rise in Europe of the 10-horned beast of Revelation—the Antichrist and his kingdom. I will be showing that events have been occurring that appear to indicate the prophecies are being fulfilled. And most Christians haven't noticed.

Watch Your Fingers, It's Alive!

o o o o o o o o o o o o o o o o o o o o o o o o o o o o o o o o
...a crisis in the Mediterranean area leads to the formation of the revived Roman Empire composed of a ten-nation confederacy.[5]

—*John F. Walvoord, 1967*

The first Gulf War crisis was the spark that re-ignited Europe's interest in the long inactive Western European Union. Iraq invaded and was occupying Kuwait. America was asking its allies for help. It frustrated the European leaders to find out how little they could do. After a long period of dormancy, the WEU began coming back to life.

As members of NATO, these European leaders were not allowed to project military power off the continent of Europe. And by themselves, these European nations were military pigmies.

According to a *Los Angeles Times* report, this is when Europe decided to bring the dormant WEU back to life. I was reminded of what John Walvoord said. He said a crisis in the Mediterranean area would lead to a ten-nation confederacy in Europe.[6]

But after the American-led Coalition forces kicked Saddam Hussein out of Kuwait, things in the Mediterranean began to calm down. America's overwhelming military victory brought a new political reality to the region. Before the Gulf War, there was a general feeling of distrust for America among the Arab leaders. They didn't like the way America supported Israel, and so they naturally resented any American military presence in the area.

But when President Bush accomplished in the Gulf War exactly what he had promised—the liberation of Kuwait—their opinions about America changed. After many long years of disbelieving the motives of the Western world, the Arab leaders were finally willing to accept America as an honest broker. And in October 1991, at the Madrid Conference, these Arab leaders sat down with Israel and began to talk about peace.

Now, once again, information on the WEU became almost impossible for me to find. It was as if those evil spiritual forces in the "mystery of lawlessness" had gone back to sleep. Soon my interest shifted away from the 10-horned beast of Revelation and the WEU. My attention returned to the first great sign of the woman—Israel and the Middle East.

Chapter 5 Notes

1. Alfred H. Burton, *The Future of Europe; Religiously and Politically, In The Light of Holy Scripture*, 4th ed. (London, Alfred Holness:1915) 14–15.

2. Charles C. Ryrie, *The Bible and Tomorrow's News* (USA: Scripture Press Publications, 1969) 35–7.

3. Clarence Larkin, *Dispensational Truth*, 122.

4. *New American Standard Bible*, 2 Thessalonians 2:7.

5. John F. Walvoord, *The Nations in Prophecy*, 103.

6. Ibid.

6

The First Overlooked Sign: The 1992 Israeli Election

The Presidential Snub

What first caught my attention was the way President George Bush, Sr., treated Israeli Prime Minister Yitzhak Shamir when he visited Washington early in 1992. Bush refused to meet with the man. Imagine how Shamir must have felt. He was being snubbed by the most powerful man in the world. Bush was the one person able to pull the bickering nations of the world together to liberate Kuwait. His popularity was so high from the Gulf War victory that none of the major names in the Democratic Party dared to risk challenging him in the coming election. And now he was publicly snubbing the Prime Minister of Israel. Why?

America's Bottom Line

I should have known. It was over oil. The bottom line of the Bush administration's foreign policy toward the Middle East was the free flow of Arab oil. Bush was from Texas and had spent many years in the oil business. Yet the oil business was not his only concern in the Middle East. The free flow of Arab oil was also seen as a legitimate concern to America's security.

A few years later, in August 1995, a scientist named Joseph P. Riva, Jr., submitted a report to Congress supporting President Bush's concern about America's need for the free flow of Arab oil. He concluded that, if the world oil demand were not to increase too much, and political stability were to continue in the Middle East so as not to interrupt the production of oil, it would be business as usual into much of the 21st century. But if not—if anything were to disturb the free flow of Arab oil, such as a war in the Middle East—America would be in for a real economic crisis.[1]

So, fearing another war in the Middle East, the Bush administration told Israel they had to negotiate peace with their Arab neighbors or lose America's support. Congress backed up the threat by not granting Israel the loan guarantees they needed to buy new jet fighters.

Thanks to the Gulf War victory, Secretary of State James Baker was making real progress with the Arabs in the renewed peace process. One man, however, was standing in the way. That man was Israeli Prime Minister Yitzhak Shamir.

Shamir became a problem for Washington because of his party's Greater Israel policy. The Greater Israel policy meant the Israeli government had no intention of giving back any of the land the Israeli army had captured from the Arabs in the Six Day War of 1967. In fact, the Shamir government was encouraging Jewish settlers to build communities in the territories the Israeli army had captured.

The problem with Shamir's Greater Israel policy was that these Jewish settlements were in direct violation of UN Resolution 242. This resolution called for Israel to give back the rest of the land they had captured in the war in exchange for peace.

Yet, the Shamir's Likud Party leaders held, in their Jewish mind, a biblical view. They saw the lands they had captured in the Six Day War as God-given and rightfully theirs. And they considered the outside world hostile to the Jewish people and saw any negotiations with the Arabs as a "slippery slope" that would ultimately lead to Israel's destruction. In other words, Shamir's government didn't think peace was possible.[2]

Since the heart of Baker's negotiations with the Arabs was implementation of UN Resolution 242, Shamir's Greater Israel policy was making any final peace agreement impossible. The Bush administration decided that the solution to their problem was to get rid of Shamir. And they saw an opportunity to do this in the approaching 1992 Israeli election. Although Shamir's conservative Likud party had managed to hold on to power for the last 15 years, the Israeli people were becoming increasingly desperate for peace. This meant the Labor Party had a good chance to win.

Shamir's challenger in the election was Yitzhak Rabin, a member of the liberal Labor Party. They agreed with the Lukid Party about the importance of security, but they rejected the Likud party's biblical view against pursuing peace with the Arabs. Their platform envisioned "a new Middle East, in which there will be no wars or terrorism."[3] So Rabin was willing to take more risks for peace than Shamir was, even if it meant giving back some of the land Israel had captured in the Six Day War.

Yet what made Rabin's challenge so serious was the fact that Rabin was a war hero. He had commanded the Israeli army that had been so successful in the Six Day War. In fact, Rabin was given much credit for the victories that led to the liberation and unification of Jerusalem and the expanded new territories. Yet there were other reasons Rabin was respected.

Besides his military experience, Rabin had already served once as a Prime Minister. And in June 1976, Rabin ordered the very successful raid that rescued a group of Air France hostages being held at an airport in Idi Amin's Uganda. The operation was so spectacular it was made into the movie, *Raid at Entebbe.*

So, now in this election, a national war hero was challenging Shamir's Greater Israel policy. Unlike Shamir, Rabin thought peace with the Arabs was possible. In fact, the territories Rabin's troops captured during the Six Day War were the same territories the UN was asking Israel to give back to the Arabs in exchange for peace. Many Israelis trusted Rabin, so when the time came when he decided to trade land for peace, most were willing to go along with him. Not even Rabin's political rivals in the Likud Party, who didn't want to trade land for peace, ever questioned Rabin's motives or his courage.

The polls showed that the voters in Israel were deeply split. On the one side, they wanted the peace the Labor Party was promising; on the other, they wanted the security the Likud Party had been providing them for the past 15 years. Rabin's Labor party correctly gauged the feelings of the Israeli voters. Their platform held out the possibility that the Israeli people could have both—peace with security. And their peace with security policies were more in line with what Washington wanted.

So this was the reason Shamir got the presidential snub when he visited Washington. And this was the reason Congress refused Israel the loan guarantees. I wasn't the only one who noticed the snub. The Israeli people noticed it, too. And it frightened them. But that's exactly what the Bush administration had been hoping for. Why?

Because even the slightest suggestion that Israel could lose America's full support was frightening to the Israeli people. Without America, Israel would be alone in the world. And for their little country to continue to survive in their hostile neighborhood, they needed ongoing American support. The presidential snub against Shamir may have been all it took to encourage Israeli voters to elect Rabin.

Later, some Middle Eastern analysts said that Washington had orchestrated the 1992 Israeli election. And this election proved to be the turning point in the Middle East peace process. Soon after Rabin's Labor Party came into power,

Israel began trying to trade the land they had captured in the Six Day War for peace.

The Overlooked Sign

o o o o o o o o o o o o o o o o o o o o o o o o o o o o o o o o o o

While they are saying, 'Peace and safety!,' then destruction will come upon them suddenly like birth pangs upon a woman with child; and they shall not escape.[4]

—*Apostle Paul, A.D. 50*

Remember, I said an important overlooked sign about the coming Antichrist may have occurred in 1992? I believe the sign occurred during this 1992 Israeli election. The reason I believe this is because of something the Apostle Paul said:

> Now as to the times and the epochs, brethren, you have no need of anything to be written to you. For you yourselves know full well that the day of the Lord will come just like a thief in the night. While they are saying, 'Peace and safety!' then destruction will come upon them suddenly like birth pangs upon a woman with child; and they shall not escape (1 Thessalonians 5:1–3).

In order for me to show you the sign, I need to first provide you with some background. In the verse mentioned above, we must remember that Paul was writing this to first-century Christians. By saying, "you yourselves know full well," we can infer that Paul was reminding his readers about some commonly accepted view the early church had about prophecy.

At this time, the book of Revelation had not yet been written. The main book for the study of prophecy in Paul's day was the Old Testament book of Daniel. And the fact that Jesus quoted much from the book of Daniel caused the early Christians to take the book and its prophecies seriously.

I believe Paul was reminding his readers of a passage from Daniel about the Antichrist coming and making a security agreement with Israel. Daniel said:

> And he (the Antichrist) will make a firm covenant with the many for one week, but in the middle of the week he will put a stop to sacrifice and grain offering; and on the wings of abominations will come one who makes desolate, even until a complete destruction, one that is decreed, is poured out on the one who makes desolate (Daniel 9:27).

As we have learned from our keys, the prophecies in Daniel are mainly concerned with Israel, the surrounding nations and the Messiah. So when Paul said, "While they are saying 'Peace and safety!' then sudden destruction will come upon them," Paul was talking about unbelieving Israel and the coming of the one who will cause the destruction. In other words, while Israel is saying "Peace and safety," then the Antichrist will come with his false security agreement.

Now coming back to the sign that may have begun occurring in the 1992 Israeli election. Paul's words, "Peace and safety" can also correctly be translated from the Greek as "Peace with security." [5] And this was what was being offered to the Israeli people in the 1992 election. When the Israeli people voted for Rabin, they were rejecting Shamir's old policies of security without peace and accepting the Labor Party's new polices of pursuing peace—peace with security.

You see, in that election the Israeli people actually began saying "Peace and safety!" by voting for Yitzhak Rabin's peace with security policies. And, if you listen, you'll notice that every following administration has been saying it to this day. This 1992 election marked the turning point in the Middle East peace process. The Israeli people began accepting the implementation of UN Resolution 242—trading land for peace. It started Israel down the dangerous road of trading land for peace, leading them to the precarious situation in which they find themselves today. This has set the stage for the coming seven-year security agreement with the Antichrist.

Rabin's victory secured Israel's acceptance of the American-sponsored peace process that had its beginning at the Madrid Conference. That following year, in 1993, Rabin signed the Oslo Accords that started Israel down that "slippery slope" that the Shamir government so feared—the road of trading land for peace. In October 1994, Rabin signed a treaty with Jordan and, in December, he was awarded the Noble Peace Prize. Then, at a peace rally in November 1995, Yizhak Rabin was assassinated.

I was touched as I studied the life of Rabin. Although he is gone, his cries for peace in the Middle East refuse to die. Unfortunately, many in modern Israel no longer even believe in prayer. Yet, as a Christian, I can't help but cry out to God for the peace of Jerusalem.

And the more I think about it, the more I believe a prophetic road sign in history occurred in that Israeli election in 1992. In that election, the majority of the Israeli people actually began saying, "Peace and safety!" And, as I have said, this election marked a daring turn in the Middle East peace process—trading land for peace. Yet, if I'm right, and this was a prophetic road sign in history, then the implications for Israel and our world are frightening. According to the Apostle

Paul, instead of the peace the Israeli people so desperately cry out for, "sudden destruction" is on its way.

In other words, the beast of Revelation is soon to rise from the sea.

Chapter 6 Notes

1. United States Government (1995, August 18) "World Oil Production After Year 2000: Business As Usual or Crises?" [Report for Congress] Joseph P. Riva, Jr., #35–925 SPR, Washington D. C.: *The National Council for Science and the Environment*, Internet: http://www.cnie.org/nle.

2. Gerald M. Steinberg, "A Nation That Dwells Along? Foreign Policy in the 1992 Election," *Professor Gerald M. Steinberg's Web site*, Internet: http://faculty.biu.ac.il/~steing/index.shtml.

3. Ibid.

4. *New American Standard Bible*, 1 Thessalonians 5:3.

5. Joseph H. Thayer, trans., *Thayer's Greek-English Lexicon*, 82.

7

Now Appearing, Those 10 Horns of Bible Prophecy

o o o o o o o o o o o o o o o o o o o o o o o o o o o o o o o o o o

First, there will appear a confederacy of ten kingdoms within the ancient Roman Empire which will constitute the first phase of its revival.[1]

—*John F. Walvoord, 1967*

If this Israeli election was the overlooked sign I suspected it to be, then I knew the Antichrist would soon be appearing on the world scene with his false security agreement with Israel.

Yet the prophecies indicate that 10 kings will appear on the world stage before the Antichrist. If you recall Daniel said, "While I was contemplating the (10) horns, behold another horn (the Antichrist), a little one, came up among them" (Daniel 7:8). This clearly indicates the 10 horns will come first.

When you think about it, it makes sense that if a beast with horns were rising from the sea, its horns would appear before its head. And this is the way it happened.

Once again the mystery of lawlessness went to work. As I said before, in January 1995, the beast of Revelation may have matured to its full set of horns—Greece officially became the 10th Member State in the Western European Union. This meant that the Brussels Treaty Powers I had been watching were now an alliance of 10 European nations. Needless to say, for a student of Bible prophecy, this could be another very important historical event—another prophetic road sign.

Especially since this event occurred just three years after the Israeli people began saying, "Peace and Safety." Taken together, this made the 10 nations that made up the Brussels Treaty Powers good candidates for becoming the 10 kings of prophecy. Not only did this alliance of European nations have the right number, but it also appeared at just the right time.

And, when we apply King Nebuchadnezzar's dream about a statue of a man as an overlay, we find a perfect match to modern Europe. Daniel described what the king saw by saying, "the feet and toes, partly of potter's clay and partly of iron, it will be a divided kingdom; but it will have in it, the toughness of iron, inasmuch as you saw the iron mixed with common clay. And as the toes of the feet were partly of pottery, so some of the kingdom will be strong and part of it will be brittle" (Daniel 2:41–42).

This strange mixture of nations is exactly what we see in the reunification process going on in modern Europe. Some of these European nations uniting together today in the European Union have in them the "toughness of iron," such as the United Kingdom and France. These countries both have strong militaries and are nuclear powers. Others are very "brittle," such as Luxembourg and Sweden. Yet, in the European Union's recent decision to create their own military capacity, taken together, these nations are on their way to becoming as strong as iron.

Yet modern Europe's match to Nebuchadnezzar's dream is even more detailed. Daniel described more of what the king saw. He said, "And in that you saw the iron mixed with common clay, they will combine with one another in the seed of men; but they will not adhere to one another, even as iron does not combine with pottery" (Daniel 2:43).

Many prophecy students have speculated about the meaning of Daniel's statement that these European nations "will combine with one another in the seed of men." Over the years, I've heard many suggestions as to what this "seed of men" will be that binds these nations together.

Yet once again, I believe the answer is simple. The "seed of men" Daniel was referring to is the common heritage these people of the European nations share with each other and the United States. In Europe, this common heritage is often referred to in speeches and documents.

For example, the first man to hold the office of High Representative for the European Union is a man by the name of Javier Solana. In June 1999, when Solana was still the Secretary General of NATO, he referred to this common heritage. He said:

Just two months ago, NATO commemorated its 50th anniversary—and the Allies, old and new, gathered in Washington to reaffirm their commitment to the principles enshrined in the North Atlantic Treaty. They reaffirmed their determination to safeguard the freedom, common heritage and civilization of their peoples, founded on the principles of democracy, individual liberty and the rule of law.[2]

Once again, Bible prophecy may have accurately revealed history before it happened. Today the European Union looks just like the feet and toes of Nebuchadnezzar's statue. It is made up of many nations, some strong like iron and others very brittle. They remain separate nations, but are bound together in a union caused by their common heritage.

Now it appears that 10 nations are emerging from these many nations, like the toes on the statue. These 10 nations are a military alliance. As we have already learned, "horns" signify "power" in prophecy. So this also qualifies these 10 nations as candidates for becoming the 10 horns on the beast seen by both Daniel and John.

Yes, indeed, modern Europe fits the overlay of Nebuchadnezzar's statue perfectly. And the 10 nations that make up the Brussels Treaty Powers could very well become the foretold 10 kings of Bible prophecy.

If so, those wicked spiritual forces that make up the mystery of lawlessness are finally making headway. And the beast of Revelation (the Antichrist) may be on his way.

The Little Horn with the Big Mouth

o o o o o o o o o o o o o o o o o o o o o o o o o o o o o o o o o o o

Second, there will appear a strong man who will consolidate these ten nations into a united kingdom and probably extend its borders in various directions.[3]

—*John F. Walvoord, 1967*

If these Brussels Treaty Powers are to become the 10 kings referred to in Bible prophecy, then one man is destined to become their leader.

The Apostle John described the relationship that will exist between these 10 kings and the Antichrist by saying, "And the ten horns which you saw are ten kings, who have not yet received a kingdom, but they receive authority as kings with the beast for one hour. These have one purpose and they give their power and authority to the beast" (Revelation 17:12–13).

By these words, it again appears that these 10 kings are in some kind of position of power before the Antichrist. These kings will be a coalition of the willing. They will willingly transfer what power and authority they have achieved together over to the Antichrist.

But this 10-horned beast won't last long. The reason it won't last is because it's going to pick on the wrong guy. John said, "These (the 10 kings and the Antichrist) will wage war against the Lamb, and the Lamb will overcome them, because He is Lord of Lords and King of Kings, and those who are with Him are the called and the chosen and faithful" (Revelation 17:14).

How could these earthly kings wage war against the Lamb who is in heaven? Actually, they can't directly. They must do it indirectly. They will turn the full weight of their world government against anything on earth that represents, in any way, the true God of heaven.

They will violate their security agreement with Israel (Daniel 9:27, 2 Thessalonians 2:3–4), they will promote a wicked false religion, and they will kill anyone who doesn't think what they are doing is wonderful (Revelation 13:13–15).

Then, like the atheistic creatures they really are, when these 10 kings and the Antichrist are finished using their false religion for their own purposes, they will destroy that, too (Revelation 17:16). Then the only power left will be theirs. Nothing on earth will be able to challenge their authority—nothing except the powers of heaven.

Chapter 7 Notes

1. John F. Walvoord, *The Nations in Prophecy*, 89.

2. Javier Solana (1999, June 21) "16th International NATO Workshop," [speech] *NATO*, Internet: http://www.nato.int.

3. Walvoord, *The Nations in Prophecy*, 89.

8

Introducing Mr. Europe

o o o o o o o o o o o o o o o o o o o o o o o o o o o o o o o

The time will come when the nations of Europe will say to one man,
'You take authority over us.' [1]

—*J. Dwight Pentecost, 1961*

As I said before, if those 10 European nations known as the Brussels Treaty Powers are to become the 10 kings of Bible prophecy, then I knew one man would soon rise to a place of power alongside them. So I began watching for the creation of an office within the European Union that could accommodate such a person. This happened with the signing of the Amsterdam Treaty in 1997.

Europe needed one voice to speak for the many nations that made up the European Union. They also needed someone to help the Council of the European Union in matters relating to their new Common Foreign and Security Policy (CFSP). The EU nations had big ambitions in this area. What they needed was someone who the world could call "Mr. Europe."[2] So, at Amsterdam, the 15 EU heads of state met together and decided to create the new office of High Representative for Common Foreign and Security Policy.

Although the Amsterdam Treaty was signed in 1997, it didn't become effective until May 1999. Then just five months later, on October 15, 1999, a remarkable man became the first to hold this office. He was a 56-year-old Spaniard by the name of Javier Solana Madariaga. He was a member of the Spanish Socialist Party and had been the prior head of NATO.

Solana's position as High Representative also made him the Secretary General of the Council of the Europe Union. The Council is one of the three main governmental institutions that make up the EU. The other two institutions are the European Parliament and the European Commission. Although the Commission is thought to be the seat of power in the EU, many experts on European affairs believe the Council of the European Union holds the real reins of power in the EU.[3]

The reason for this is because the General Secretariat in the Council of Europe provides continuity to the policies being worked on by the EU's rotating presidents. The 15 heads of the member states take turns at being president every six months. In other words, the EU presidents are only there for six months at a time. This hardly allows them time to get much done.

This is why the Council Secretariat is there to help them. With him, as the EU presidents come and go, the work in the Council can continue uninterrupted. The Secretary General of the Council—the office Solana was appointed to for a five-year term—administers the Council Secretariat. So when you add the office of High Representative to the office of Secretary General of the Council, you make Solana a very powerful man in the EU.

I wasn't the only one thinking that Solana had been given tremendous power. In an official document for the Western European Union, Antonio Missiroli said that Solana's combined positions could threaten the EU presidency itself. His warning was in the Chaillot Paper #38 for the Institute for Security Studies of the WEU. Missiroli said:

> Finally, Javier Solana's appointment as EU Council Secretary-General and High Representative (SG/HR) for the CFSP is expected to foster coordination and consistency...however [Solana's appointment], may also create a dualism with the presidency of the Union and, more generally, tensions within the new EU troika: in fact, the democratic element represented by the rotational presidency may be easily offset by the SG/HR...And here, predictably, the balance of power and influence will change according to the size, political weight and specific attitude of the country holding the presidency—including whether it belongs or not to the above-mentioned 'core' [the 10 Brussels Treaty Powers].[4]

Here, we once again find the 10 Brussels Treaty Powers. Missiroli referred to these nations in his paper as the "core." The implication of his remarks is that these so-called "core" nations carry more weight in the EU than the others. This was when I began to realize how unstable the politics in the EU were compared to the United States. Missiroli seemed to be saying that, now that Solana was on the scene, nobody knew for sure what was going to happen next in the EU.

Then on November 25 1999, while American was about to celebrate Thanksgiving Day, something big did happen—something even I wasn't expecting. Solana's already lofty position was made even more powerful. Solana put on his third hat and became the Secretary General of the WEU military alliance. In other words, Solana had now been placed in a position of influence over those "core" 10 Brussels Treaty Powers. He now was the head of Europe's exclusive military club.

I was shocked by this news. The prophetic implications of this event were many. I knew if the Brussels Treaty Powers were to become the 10 kings of prophecy, then one man with influence in the EU would rise to power among them. And this had just happened.

In fact, it was this event that caused me to write the column about Solana that Constance Cumbey read when she decided to give me a call. Needless to say, these three positions—High Representative, Secretary General of the Council of Europe, and now Secretary General of the WEU—made Solana an extremely powerful player in the EU. This would make him—or someone who is to hold his office in the future—a good candidate for the Antichrist.

Solana was not only the head of the most powerful agency in the EU (the Council of the European Union), but he was also the one entrusted with creating and directing Europe's new Common Foreign and Security Policy. And now he was also in tight with those 10 core nations.

Alone, these events were significant. Taken together, they were astounding. It was becoming impossible for me to ignore what was going on in Europe as indications that the Bible prophecies were about to be fulfilled. In other words, I was becoming convinced that "signs of the times" were again occurring in our world. And once again they seemed to be going unnoticed.

Javier Who?

Referring to the Antichrist, *Willmington's Guide to the Bible* states:

He will be an intellectual genius (Daniel 8:23). He will be an oratorical genius (Daniel11:36). He will be a political genius (Revelation 17:11–12). He will be a commercial genius (Revelation 13:16, Daniel 11:43). He will be a military genius (Revelation 6:2, 13:2). He will be a religious genius (Revelation 13:8).[5] So, could Javier Solana actually be the first to hold the office the Antichrist will someday hold? This idea was too bizarre to be believable. Yet I was looking for a Mr. Europe to come on the scene and, now that I'd found one, I didn't know what to do with him. I decided to learn all I could about this first Mr. Europe—Javier Solana.

Since Solana was the former head of NATO, I figured he must have done a good job. If he hadn't, then he wouldn't have been given such a key position in the development of the EU's new foreign policy. I was right.

Javier Solana became the Secretary General of the NATO Alliance in 1995. A nasty scandal in the organization had left the Western leaders groping to find a new head for NATO that everyone would like. Whoever this person turned out to be, he would have an important job. He would have to restructure NATO to face the realities of the post-Cold War.

There was also an immediate problem in the Balkans to deal with. The United States didn't want to commit ground troops to the region, and NATO was preparing for air strikes. The job waiting for the new head of NATO would be no cakewalk.

The American Secretary of State Warren Christopher had learned to appreciate the diplomatic skills of Javier Solana while Solana was a Foreign Minister in Spain. Christopher recommended Solana to President Clinton, and Clinton took Christopher's advice.[6]

Although most of the Western leaders liked the idea, Solana's appointment came as quite a surprise. The reason for their surprise was that, as a youth, Solana had participated in anti-NATO demonstrations in Spain. In fact, Solana's leftist political activism had been so extreme that he was expelled from Madrid's Complutense University in 1963.[7]

Ironically, it was to this grown-up radical from the 1960s—a person who had once described himself as a pragmatic Marxist—that the Western leaders gave the job of restructuring NATO for the new post-Cold War era.

Under Solana's supervision, the number of NATO headquarters was reduced from 65 to 20. The remaining headquarters were divided into two Strategic Commands—one for the Atlantic and another for Europe. It was as if NATO was split right down the middle.[8]

Solana's restructuring made room for NATO expansion, an important part of the Western leaders' plans for the post-Cold War era. These leaders felt that NATO had done such a good job in Europe that the benefits of the alliance should be offered to other parts of Europe, and even possibly to the whole world.[9]

What made the NATO alliance so desirable was the fact that it was only open to democratic governments with open markets. For a nation to join NATO it had to first meet these requirements.

Another desirable result of NATO expansion was the lessening of the chance for war. NATO members don't go to war against each other.

Yet expansion was not the only reason NATO needed to be restructured. The Western leaders wanted to make it possible for the European nations to use NATO's military assets without America's participation. In other words, the EU wanted its own independent military capacity.

The war in Bosnia had once again driven home to the European leaders just how weak they really were. They first realized this during the Gulf War, and now they were facing their military impotence again.

So Solana was given quite a job as the new head of NATO. Not only did he have to win the war in Bosnia, but he also had to restructure NATO for the post-Cold War era. With this restructuring, the Western leaders wanted to make possible their dreams for a new pan-European security arrangement that, if properly shaped, could possibly go global. This was no small task.

Yet I couldn't help but wonder: Why would we Americans want to make NATO resources available to our European allies for their independent use? I realized that something big was happening in Europe that the American people didn't know about. The balance of military power that had existed for the last 50 years in America's favor was going to change. Europe was on its way to once again becoming a military power. And they were going to do it with our equipment and help.

Again I ask, why would American want this to happen—let alone help it happen? Perhaps the best man in the Clinton administration to answer that question was the Deputy Secretary of State Strobe Talbott. In July 1992, he wrote an essay for *Time* magazine titled, "The Birth of the Global Nation," where he revealed that he believed global government is inevitable.

The following year after the essay was published, he took his post as Deputy Secretary General under the Clinton administration and helped shape the Clinton foreign policy from the very beginning.

In the same essay, Talbott said about federalism, "If that model does indeed work globally, it would be the logical extension of the Founding Fathers' wisdom, therefore a special source of pride for a world government's American constituents." [10]

To me it seems likely that Talbott's views on federalism may have greatly influenced President Clinton and contributed to the idea of NATO expansion as a model for the New World Order.

So the Western leaders got together and decided to make NATO a model for their new post-Cold War security scheme. As I thought about this, I realized that NATO expansion was, in reality, an attempt to create a new pan-European security arrangement and, if possible, a New World Order.

In fact, Solana said so himself. On January 11, 1999, he said:

> Today, NATO and the EU stand as the world's foremost models of multinational, democratic cooperation. They exert a tremendous attractiveness to the many nations who aspire to join or cooperate with them. Both organizations have inspired the larger European project of integration, of cooperation and reconciliation which is healing the unnatural divide of the past between East and West. They are thus both leaders of the drawing together of Europe, its rejuvenation and reconstruction. We must keep firmly in our sights this higher political project that both organizations, in their own respective ways, embody. Just as the European Union is more than a common market, but the embodiment of a political ideal, so too NATO is more than a military alliance for the collective defense of its members. It is a symbol of how countries can strive together for peace, security and stability across a whole continent.[11]

While head of NATO, Solana was given the credit for holding the bickering allies together during the long bombing campaign directed against Serbia—something many didn't think could be done.

But what most caught the approving eyes of the European leaders was the fact that Solana was personally responsible for talking Russia into allowing the NATO expansion. This expansion was something the Western leaders very much desired. Yet few in diplomatic circles thought Russia could ever be talked into letting former East Block countries become members of their rival military organization. But this is what Solana succeeded in doing.

It was reported that—after Solana worked out this agreement with Russia—he received a standing ovation at NATO headquarters in Brussels. The Western leaders credited Solana's diplomacy for making possible the biggest change to Europe's security since the Yalta Conference reshaped Europe at the end of World War II.[12]

But something Solana said near the end of his term as head of NATO should have shocked these Western leaders. In a moment of reflection, Solana actually referred to someone—possibly himself—as the "Head of the International Community." At a press conference in Pristina, Kosovo, Solana said:

> A good part of my 4 years tenure as Secretary General of NATO has been devoted to the Balkans and a good part devoted to Kosovo. You can image with what emotion I am here today in Pristina for the last time in this capacity. The challenges that lie ahead are immense. The tremendous tragedy of Kosovo has been lived by many of you and many of us, but I think with good will, with co-operation, with the visions of so many leaders here in Europe

and in the world, the Head of the International Community, with all that, we will create the ingredients to create a new future for the population living here. You can be sure that I will continue in my new capacity as High Representative of Foreign and Security policy in the European Union, to engage which for me is part of my life already.[13]

Constance Cumbey brought Solana's comment to my attention. She calls this press conference Solana's "Head of the World" speech. And her point is well taken. Who did Solana mean when he referred to the "Head of the International Community?" Was he referring to himself or to someone else?

No matter how much we choose to read into Solana's words at that press conference one thing is clear—big changes are occurring to the balance of power on the European continent. And Javier Solana is right in the middle of them.

Going Our Way?

o o o o o o o o o o o o o o o o o o o o o o o o o o o o o o o o o

The resulting prosperity of Europe under this arrangement has brought forth many predictions of an ultimate United States of Europe which could eventually include not only Europe itself, but the Mediterranean world.[14]

—*John F. Walvoord, 1967*

Just as I had become interested in the 10 Brussels Treaty Powers and the WEU, now I was interested in a man by the name of Javier Solana. As I thought about all this, I recalled the election in Israel that may have been a sign indicating the rise of the Antichrist. If Solana was the first to hold the office the Antichrist would someday hold, then a security agreement with Israel must already be in the works. Solana and the Brussels Treaty Powers would have some kind of connection to the Middle East. I soon found out they did—and in a big way.

Javier Solana was the first name I saw listed on the Barcelona Declaration. This document was adopted by the Council of Europe on November 1995 at a conference held in Madrid, Spain. The agreement created the Euro-Mediterranean Partnership for Peace. It established a large area of cooperation—including a free trade area—between the member states of the EU and twelve Mediterranean nations, including Israel.[15]

What interested me about the Euro-Mediterranean Partnership for Peace was that this kind of agreement was used to create the EU. It first began as a free-trade area known for a time as the Common Market. Gradually these nations began to integrate more deeply. Today, these European nations are hip-deep in a mire of confusing treaties binding them together in what has become known as the modern European Union.

In a persuasive speech, "Sleepwalking into the European Superstate," an Englishman by the name of Sir James Goldsmith compared the current unification process going on in Europe to the events that created war-loving Prussia in 1834. Prussia gained control over her neighboring countries by first creating a free-trade area. From there, step by step, the nations lost their sovereignty to the Prussian bureaucrats.

His speech was given as a warning. Goldsmith believes that the EU may be headed in the same direction as Prussia. Since the EU began as a free trade area—the European Common Market—Goldsmith believes the EU bureaucrats in Brussels could be using the same ploy as Prussia did to create a European Superstate.[16]

And part of the plans for the Superstate apparently include the Mediterranean since the EU is now attempting to extend its free trade area there. If their plans are successful, then once again the map of Europe would appear as it did during the time of Christ. The shadow of the Roman Empire would once again fall across Israel. And the ancient prophecies found in the Bible would again prove true.

As I mentioned, Javier Solana was the first name mentioned on the Barcelona Declaration. This agreement began a process of cooperation to create free trade between the 15 EU nations and the 12 Mediterranean nations—including Israel.

As a Foreign Minister in Spain, Solana held the rotating presidency of the Council of Europe the year of the Madrid Conference in 1995. He was very much involved with the details of the negotiations. We know this because Solana was credited with a bit of last-minute diplomacy during the conference that saved the day. When Syria and Israel were not able to come together on a sensitive issue, Solana came up with a compromise both nations were able to agree to.[17]

So Solana's connection to the Middle East was established. He was personally playing a big role in the development of the EU's foreign policy regarding the Mediterranean. I wondered how much more about this modern rebirth of the Roman Empire could be traced to Javier Solana. And I wondered how much more I was going to find linking Solana to Israel and the prophecies of the Bible. It was almost getting scary.

Solana's Maniac Mandate

o o o o o o o o o o o o o o o o o o o o o o o o o o o o o o o o

His god will be the god of fortresses. The antichrist will spend all his resources on military programs.[18]

—*H. L. Willmington, 1981*

o o o o o o o o o o o o o o o o o o o o o o o o o o o o o o o o

This man will appear as a savior and deliverer. He will bring peace to world tension by settling the Arab-Israeli dispute by his united power.[19]

—*J. Dwight Pentecost, 1961*

It was no surprise that the 15 EU heads of state chose Solana to be their first High Representative, Secretary General of the Council of Europe, and Secretary General of the WEU. With his past experience as the head of NATO and his amazing diplomatic skills, he was the perfect man to implement the Western leaders new pan-European security scheme.

Without Solana's personal intervention, Russia may never have agreed to NATO's eastward expansion. And without Russia's approval, the European leaders' new security plans would have been dangerous—if not impossible—to proceed with.

And here is where things started to get really prophetically interesting. A European Council's decision at Helsinki gave Solana a mandate to create an independent army for the European Union by 2003.[20] The EU heads of state, however, didn't like calling it an army. They preferred to call it a military "capacity." The difference being, instead of a standing army, they were creating a "capacity" to draw forces from member states when needed. They also like to point out that the 15 nations that make up the EU do not have a mutual defense policy. They say NATO is available to the member states for this purpose.

Yet no matter what they called it, everybody knew the EU was creating a European army. In fact, when Romano Prodi, the president of the European Commission, was jumped for using the "A-word," he snapped back: "When I was talking about the European army, I wasn't joking. If you don't want to call it a

European army, don't call it a European army. You can call it 'Margaret', you can call it 'Mary Ann', you can call it any name."[21]

The official spin from Brussels was that the EU's new military capacity would consist of 60,000 troops drawn from the member states. It was to be deployable for up to one year on a short notice. This force was only to be used for humanitarian and peacekeeping missions. Although Solana was told to have the force ready by 2003, he had only until the end of 2000 to work out the details.

Yet the Helsinki Council decision not only mandated that an independent military force be created, but it also called for the establishment of a "full range of crisis management capabilities." What this meant was that they also wanted Solana to establish non-military capacities. This non-military aspect would consist of civilian agencies that could distribute aid and disaster relief. It would also include a 5,000-officer paramilitary police force.

Like I said, this is where things got interesting. The EU heads of state wanted Solana to create a super police force to make and maintain world peace. According to Bible prophecy, this is how the Antichrist will rise to power—through a false peace program (Daniel 8:25).

The EU calls their missions to bring peace Petersberg Tasks. They identified these so-called Petersberg Tasks as humanitarian and rescue tasks, peacekeeping, crises management and peacemaking. And, they don't plan on limiting these forces to the continent of Europe. They plan on deploying them anywhere in the world where they believe their interests are threatened.

A civil liberties organization in Europe, Statewatch, shares my concerns about the EU's so-called Petersberg Tasks. In December 2000, they posted an online article, "Global 'Policing' Role for EU." At the conclusion of the article they said:

> The distinction between the 'defense' of the EU (which is defined as NATO's job) and 'peacekeeping [and] peacemaking' is quite spurious. There are genuine humanitarian situations where all the resources of the EU should be used to save lives and there are also some situations where the UN has authorized military interventions (controversial and otherwise). But the idea that the EU should act independently (so-called 'autonomous') in military or 'non-military' operations raises much bigger issues as does the use of non-military crises to ensure that the EU has 'more reliable partners, more secure investments' (Solana).[22]

Consider what is being said. The reason the EU heads of state want Solana to create a military and non-military crisis management capacity is so they can force other nations into doing what they wish. Not only do they want military forces, but they also want a full range of non-military capabilities. These will include some kind of international police force.

What makes this even more frightening is that these are the kind of things the Antichrist is supposed to do in his rise to power. It is commonly believed that the Antichrist will come into his place of power through deceitful political maneuvering and false programs of peace. One reason people believe this is because of a passage in Daniel. Regarding the Antichrist Daniel said:

> And in the latter period of their rule, when the transgressors have run their course, a king will arise, insolent and skilled in intrigue. And his power will be mighty, but not by his own power, and he will destroy to an extraordinary degree, and prosper and perform his will; he will destroy mighty men and the holy people. And through his shrewdness he will cause deceit to succeed by his influence; and he will magnify himself in his heart, and he will destroy many while they are at ease. He will oppose the Prince of princes, but he will be broken without human agency (Daniel 8:23–25).

While the New American Standard Bible says, "he will destroy many while they are at ease," the King James Bible says, "and by peace shall destroy many."

And this appears to be the job description Solana has been given by the EU heads of state. He is to create for them a rapid reaction force and crisis management capacity. These combined forces are to be available for so-called Petersberg tasks—peacekeeping and peacemaking. And the EU wants these forces available anywhere in the world where its interests are threatened.

Things were getting quite interesting.

10-Horned Friend or Foe?

ο ο ο ο ο ο ο ο ο ο ο ο ο ο ο ο ο ο ο ο ο ο ο ο ο ο ο ο ο ο

The final or third stage may be in a state of partial disintegration at the time of the second coming of Christ as indicated by the very fact that there is warfare and rebellion against the Roman ruler. [23]

—*John F. Walvoord, 1967*

The creation of an independent European army brings Americans to an interesting question. In light of what we've been learning about the European Union's ambitious new foreign policy, is war with our European allies a future possibility?

Even if Americans don't think so, our allies might. According to an essay written by Carlos Masala, senior academic researcher for the Institute for Political Science and European Affairs at the University of Cologne, our European allies are already considering the possibility of such a conflict.

Masala believes a confrontation between the United States and the EU may be on the horizon because of the recent changes to the EU's foreign policy I've just mentioned—things most Americans aren't aware of.

One of the most important of these is the Euro-Mediterranean Partnership for Peace that came about because of the Barcelona Declaration. Masala acknowledges that the Barcelona Declaration is, in reality, a potentially global process for integrating other nations into the EU. The global process begins, however, with the 12 Mediterranean nations. And this could lead to problems with the United States.

As I've said before, the bottom line to America's foreign policy in the Mediterranean area is the free flow of Arab oil. This is because any interruption in the oil supply would be a crisis to the American economy. So the United States could very well consider their vital interests threatened should they see the EU's new foreign policy bearing any real fruit.

Another change that could stir up problems between the United States and Europe is the EU's determination to create an independent military, led by its own High Representative. Many experts believe these moves will destroy NATO. In fact, on December 7, 2000, the *Daily Telegraph* reported that then U.S. Secretary of Defense William Cohen warned NATO ministers that if Europe continued with its plans for an independent military, then NATO would become a "relic of the past."

By itself, the essay written by Masala would not have much importance. The problem is, his essay was published as an Occasional Paper by the Institute for Security Studies, a division of the Western European Union. In other words, this was an official paper for the 10 Brussels Treaty Powers that control the WEU and make up the EU's new military.

Regarding the "worst case scenario" that could result because of all the recent changes to EU foreign policy—specifically the Barcelona process in regards to the Mediterranean area—Carlos Masala writes: "The Mediterranean region, especially the eastern Mediterranean would become an area of competition and maybe conflict between the former allies."[24]

So, is the unthinkable occurring? Are our European allies actually preparing for a possible conflict with the United States over the Mediterranean area? To me, the official reasons Brussels is giving us for forming an EU military do become suspect in light of the Euro-Mediterranean Partnership for Peace.

What are the official reasons coming out of Brussels? That depends on the audience. In a speech Solana gave to an audience concerned about the future of EU-NATO relations, he said, "The creation of a European Security and Defense Policy is aimed at strengthening, not weakening transatlantic ties. By pulling its full weight, the European Union will contribute to transatlantic relations by better sharing the burden of security."[25]

Yet, in a speech at a Madrid university, Solana emphasized humanitarian concerns as the reason for creating an EU military. He said:

> The European Union is thus equipping itself for better crisis management…What we need now, is to supply the Union—as such—with the means and the capacity to act in the field: whether for logistic purposes; or to protect humanitarian staff and convoys; or to get access to the victims, in cases where this would otherwise prove impossible. It is why the member states of the European Union have committed themselves in Helsinki to the deployment of a force of 60,000 military personnel, to be drawn from the member states, by the year 2003.[26]

So, after 50 years of depending on the United States for security, why are our European allies suddenly willing to spend their citizens' hard earned money for an independent military capacity? They tell us it is to strengthen NATO. They also say it's because of their global humanitarian concerns. And, perhaps, we still have friends in Europe who really believe this.

But, as we've been seeing, the prophecies in the Bible indicate there may be forces at work that have other plans for the EU's new crises management capabilities. And these forces are definitely not our friends. I'm referring, of course, to those wicked spiritual forces that make up the mystery of lawlessness.

Getting Personal

Since Javier Solana has become such an important player in the EU, I wanted to find out all I could about him. Here are some of the things I learned.

He was born on July 14,1942, to an influential family in Madrid, Spain—a country bordering the Mediterranean. In his college days, he was kicked out of school because of his participation in anti-NATO demonstrations. His family managed to press the right buttons, and he was allowed to continue his education.

He earned his doctorate in physics as a Fulbright scholar at several American universities. While in America he witnessed the demonstrations over Vietnam and civil rights and looks back to these events with fondness.[27] But he was afraid to participate because he wasn't a citizen. While in America he also met and married his wife, Concepcion.

After completing his education, he and his wife moved back to Spain. Solana became a professor of solid-state physics at Madrid Complutense University. During his time there, he published more than 30 technical books on the subject.

In 1964, Solana joined the Spanish Socialist Party. From there, he rose to become a member of Parliament in 1974. When the Socialists came into power in 1982, he was appointed a Spanish Cabinet Minister. He held a Cabinet position in Spain until 1995, when he was appointed Secretary General of NATO—the organization he once tried to destroy.

And here is a bit of information that may prove important to our understanding of how the prophecies could relate to this man. Javier Solana just happens to be a member of the Spanish chapter of the Club of Rome.[28]

Chapter 8 Notes

1. J. Dwight Pentecost, *Prophecy For Today* (Grand Rapids: Zondervan Publishing House,1961) 90.

2. Peter Ford, "Now U.S. can ring up Mr. Europe," *Christian Science Monitor*, 4 June 1999, vol. 91, issue 132.

3. Derek Brown, "Who Holds the Reins of Power in Europe?," special report: EU integration, 29 November 2000, *Guardian Unlimited*, Internet: http://www.guardian.co.

4. Antonio Missiroli (2000, February) "CFSP, Defense and Flexibility" [Chaillot Paper 38] Western European Union, *Institute for Securities Studies*, Internet: http://www.weu.int.

5. H. L Willmington, *Willmington's Guide to the Bible*, 563.

6. Jay Branegan, "A Straight-Shooting Spaniard at NATO," *Time*, 13 January 1997, vol. 149 No.2, Europe.

7. Ibid.

8. "NATO Handbook," 1998 edition, NATO, Internet: http://www.nato.int

9. NATO (1999, April 24) "The Alliance's Strategic Concept" [press release], Internet: http://www.nato.int.

10. Strobe Talbott, "The Birth of the Global Nation," *Time*, 20 July 1992.

11. Javier Solana (1999, January 11) "NATO Agenda towards the Washington Summit" [speech] *NATO*, Internet: http://www.nato.int.

12. James Walsh, "A Done Deal," *Time*, 26 May 1997, vol. 149 No. 21, Europe.

13. Javier Solana, (1999, September 27) "KFOR Press Conference by the NATO Secretary General" [transcript] *NATO*, Internet: http://www.nato.int/kosovo/press/1999/k990927b.htm.

14. John F. Walvoord, *The Nations in Prophecy*, 93.

15. European Union, "Barcelona Declaration" (1995, September 27–28) *Europa*, Internet: http://www.europa.eu.int.

16. Sir. James Goldsmith (1996) "Sleepwalking into the European Superstate" [speech] *Free Britain*, Internet: http://www.freebritain.co.uk

17. Benjamin Jones, "Javier Solana," [profile] *Europe* magazine, Feb 1996, issue 353, 25,1p, 1c.

18. H. L. Willmington, *Willmington's Guide to the Bible*, 242.

19. J. Dwight Pentecost, *Prophecy For Today*, 90.

20. European Union *(1999, December 11–12)* "Helsinki European Council" [presidency conclusion] *Europa*, Internet: http://www.europa.eu.int.

21. George Kerevan, "E.U. Marching Towards a Confederation Army," *The Scotsman*, 21 November 2000, 1.

22. Statewatch News Online, "Global 'Policing' Role for EU," *Statewatch News Online*, Internet: http://www.statewatch.org.

23. John F. Walvoord, *The Nations in Prophecy*, 89.

24. Carlos Masala, "XIV. Four Scenarios for the Relationship between the EMP and NATO's Mediterranean Dialogue," published in Martin Ortega, ed. (2000, March) "The Future of the Euro-Mediterranean Security Dialogue," [Occasional Papers] Western European Union, *Institute for Security Studies*, Internet: http://www.weu.int.

25. Solana (2000, November 8) "The Foreign Policy of the EU—Liberal International—The Hague," [speech] *Europa*, Internet: http://www.europa.eu.int.

26. Solana (2000, July 7) "Inaugural Conference of the Course 'Towards a New International Morality: the Humanitarian Interventions,'" [speech] *Europa*, Internet:http://www.europa.eu.int.

27. Jay Branegan, "A Straight-Shooting Spaniard at NATO," *Time*, 13 January 1997, Vol. 149 No. 2, Europe.

28. *Europa*, Internet: http://www.europa.eu.int.

9

No Club Like Rome

○ ○

One interesting characteristic of his (the Antichrist's) coming is that he has a bow in his hand, symbolic of aggressive warfare, but no arrow, indicating that he will conquer by diplomacy rather than by war. Ushering in a false peace, he will be the superman who promises to solve all the world's problems. That he will be ultimately victorious is seen by the fact that he has a crown upon his head.[1]

—Tim Lahaye, 1975

This world ruler is going to show special antagonism against the Most High and against His saints, and he shall seek 'to change times and laws.' He is going to reject all law that had been instituted previously, and he is going to institute his own lawless system.[2]

—J. Dwight Pentecost, 1961

What people do with their spare time reveals something about their values. Some people join a church. Others join a club that shares their interests. Javier Solana joined the Spanish chapter of the Club of Rome. But this isn't just any club. It's only open, by invitation, to certain key players in our world—such as scientists and former heads of state.

What are the interests of these people who join the Club of Rome? It seems their main concern is for the creation of some form of global government. They believe that—unless we can soon establish a global government—our world may experience a sudden and uncontrollable collapse in its ability to sustain its population.[3]

It is apparent that the Club of Rome is a secular humanist organization. In fact, that's why its members want global government in the first place. Secular humanism teaches that humans are the product of evolution, not created by God. Since we can't depend on God, we must take control of our own evolutionary process to create a better world. So humanists believe global government is necessary to advance man's evolution.[4]

At the beginning of the Declaration of the Club of Rome, we find these words:

> We, the members of the Club of Rome, are convinced that the future of humankind is not determined once and for all, and that it is possible to avoid present and foreseeable catastrophes—when they are the result of human selfishness or of mistakes made in managing world affairs.[5]

As I thought about the implication of those words, I realized that the Declaration of the Club of Rome could actually be interpreted as a declaration of war against the Bible and God's people. In their declaration they say, "We, the members of the Club of Rome, are convinced that the future of humankind is not determined once for all."

But this statement is in direct opposition to what the Bible has to say. If you recall, Jesus appeared the first time to Israel on a day that had been predetermined by God (Daniel 9:24–25). And Jesus indicated to His disciples that the day He was to return the second time was also predetermined by God (Acts 1:7).

Yet the members of the Club of Rome say, in their declaration, that they are "convinced that the future of humankind is not determined once for all." Does this sound like something the Antichrist might think or say? I believe it does. In fact, this may shed light on a difficult prophecy. Regarding the Antichrist, an angel said: "And he will speak out against the Most High and wear down the saints of the Highest One, and he will intend to make alterations in times and in law; and they will be given into his hand for a time, times, and half time (3 1/2 years, Daniel 7:25).

As I read this prophecy, I realized that the Antichrist's self-serving agenda could easily be disguised behind the humanistic ideas advocated by the Club of Rome. If so, the Antichrist would attempt to abolish all knowledge of the true God and destroy God's people. He would try to evade the fulfillment of the end-times prophecies and establish a worldwide humanist paradise based on a new, godless, global ethic. And, for a period of three and a half years, God will allow him to have success.

Is creating a new, godless, global government something the members of the Club of Rome could support? I believe it might be. In a recent paper written for the Club of Rome's annual meeting, titled "Governance in an era of Globalization," we find these frightening words:

> We have come to the conclusion that the globalizing world suffers from deficits and problems that need to be solved with a sense of urge and direction. But we have also seen that states and the interstate system suffer from governmental shortcomings and democratic deficits. They can not realize the needed quality of life in the globalizing world. Thus, we need to look for governance alternatives.[6]

What exactly do the writers of this Club of Rome paper mean by saying the "states and the interstate systems suffer governmental shortcomings" and that we need to be looking for "governance alternatives?" It seems they are suggesting that our world's current independent nation states can't be trusted anymore to do the job, and so we need to replace, or supplement, them with something better.

So what is the game plan of the Club of Rome? Are they just a group of concerned global citizens who are trying to create a new, global awareness? Or could there be something a little more menacing in the works? I believe there may well be. And since Solana has control over the foreign and security policy for the EU, perhaps we should consider what his club has to say about foreign policy.

The writers of the same paper for the Club of Rome say:

> By coupling trade rules with other issues you can force countries to adopt just and sustainable production processes. If countries do not apply with a certain minimum level of, for example, labor conditions, other countries are allowed to close their borders for exports from the deviant.

Is this how Solana believes the EU's new foreign policy should be implemented? Is his purpose to bring countries into a trade agreements that later will be used against them? There is good reason to believe it is. In fact, it looks like Solana may already be following some of the suggestions made in this paper.

For example, Solana's use of the Club of Rome's "carrot and stick" approach is credited with persuading the Serbian people to vote for the recent change in their government. His "carrot" was an offer to the Balkan nations of full integration into the economies of the EU nations. His "stick" was economic and political sanctions that wouldn't go away until they complied with his wishes.

But economic sanctions aren't the only tool the Club of Rome suggests to establish their world government. The paper also suggests a supplement to our existing nation state system—the creation and implementation of some kind of new, global ethic.

They call this supplement "New Governance." The writers say:

> New governance refers to the capacity to realize societal values, while this capacity is not based on the possibility to form and enforce laws, but has strength beyond the law. New governance is not based on territorial jurisdiction, on the parliamentary approach, on a constitution and paper law, on law enforcing institutions. New governance is based on values practiced in and by societal institutions. Global new governance will ideally be based on a global ethic. The values are to be realized and the ethic internalized by both states, business and civil society.

It sounds like the Club of Rome paper is calling for the development and propagation of a new, global ethic. As a Christian, and knowing what the Bible prophecies say the Antichrist will do, I can't help but suspect they may also want to do away with the old Judeo-Christian ethic.

Does Javier Solana agree with these ideas found in the Club of Rome paper? Once more the evidence suggests that he does. Solana was invited to speak at Madrid's University of Alcala' de Henares, for the inauguration of a new class, "Towards a New International Morality; the Humanitarian Interventions."

In this speech, Solana not only reveals his support for teaching a new, global ethic, but he also reveals what this new ethic means to him—global interventions. He said:

> Looking at the activities which are at the heart of the work of this Center, I could hardly think of a more compelling subject issue than humanitarian interventions. In fact, we are talking of a very modern way to describe a very ancient practice. To help out one's fellow human being in a situation of distress, whether that situation is caused by personal circumstances, natural disaster, economic ruin or war, is a timeless and universal instinct, found in all people.[7]

Solana then went on to say that this new ethic—global interventions to help out one's fellow human being—was the reason he was creating the EU's new military. So here we find Solana giving a speech that appears to be promoting his Club of Rome's so-called "New Governance." Not only that, but he is also using the new ethics being taught by this college to supplement his own foreign policy scheme for global interventions.

Evidently, Solana realized that—for some of the more critical thinkers in his audience—his interventionist foreign policy ideas still required more justification. So he closed his speech by saying:

> Because foreign policy nowadays is, ultimately, about people, not just about States. About people who are the target of ominous conflicts; about people in need, for which Europe provides the main lifeline through humanitarian relief; about people out there—our citizens—who unreservedly support this solidarity, and value the achievements of European integration also on these grounds.

Yes, what Solana is offering the citizens of Europe certainly sounds good. The problem is, these so-called humanitarian interventions he is arming the EU to respond to are not only meant for the EU nations—they are global. Solana plans on intervening with his new military anywhere in the world he feels it's necessary. With his global humanitarian agenda in mind, in the same speech Solana said:

> Specific tasks include monitoring potential crisis areas around the globe, and assessing the needs of each situation, with a view to providing the right kind of assistance—at the right time and in the right place—as and when a crisis emerges.

I hate to think what would happen if someone like Solana was successful in implementing all the humanistic ideas for global government found in that Club of Rome paper. Yet this may actually be occurring—not only in Solana's EU Superstate, but also in Kofi Annan's recently reorganized United Nations.

I say this because one of the authors of this Club of Rome paper is Professor Ruud Lubbers. He teaches courses on Globalization Studies at both Tilburg and Harvard Universities. And guess what? The UN Secretary General Kofi Annan recently announced the appointment of Dr. Ruud Lubbers to a high-profile position within the United Nations.

As I asked before, could there be something a little more sinister going on here? If you compare Solana's plans for the creation of a rapid reaction force for Europe with Kofi Annan's plans for the creation of a rapid reaction force for the UN, they appear to be coming from the same playbook.

Could that playbook be from the Club of Rome?

The City and Tower of Babel

o o o o o o o o o o o o o o o o o o o o o o o o o o o o o o o o

The one-world government, the one-world religion, and the one-world banking system that make possible the commerce of the world are already gathering momentum. It is just a matter of time before they decide to locate in a single spot. That spot will be Babylon.[8]

—Tim Lahaye, 1975

It was a mess. 197 world leaders, each with their own motorcade, invaded New York at one time. It was the largest gathering of heads of state in history. They were there to attend the three-day Millennium Summit at the UN headquarters, starting on September 6, 2000.

Yet, the week earlier, the scene at the New York Waldorf-Astoria Hotel was even stranger. Here we had spiritual leaders representing more than 50 religions gathering together for their own summit—the World Peace Summit. In addition to Western clergy, there were African drummers, Hindu chanters and tribal holymen.

The religious gathering had been organized by a group of interfaith activists with a little help from their friends—New Age billionaire Maurice Strong and Time-Warner's chief, Ted Turner. The purpose of the gathering was to find a way the world's religious leaders could contribute to the UN's quest for world peace.

After arriving in the UN General Hall, Ted Turner took the podium. He received hoots and cheers from the audience when he detailed the reasons he denounced his childhood Christian faith, according to Austin Ruse, a professional UN observer. Darren Logan, a foreign policy analyst for the Washington-based Family Research Council, described Turner's speech as "the most blasphemous thing I have ever heard in my life."[9]

When the clamor had settled, a Declaration for World Peace had been created. It called for the establishment of an International Advisory Council of Religious and Spiritual Leaders to serve the UN in crises resolution and prevention.

The following week, the world's political leaders met in the same assembly hall. The meeting began with a moment of silence for three UN staff members who had recently been killed in East Timor. This moment of silence set the stage for UN Secretary General Kofi Annan to make his appeal to the world leaders. He asked them to support his and the Security Council's proposals to strengthen the UN's peacekeeping ability by giving them their own military forces. The UPI reported that Annan called for: "strengthening the United Nations in the crucial area of peace and security—the area where people look especially to the state, and where the world's people look to the United Nations, to save them 'from the scourge of war.'"[10]

Annan was telling these world leaders that, like it or not, their UN organization was due for a complete overhaul. In fact, at that time, Congress was already working on H.R. 4453—a bill in response to a Presidential Directive issued by Bill Clinton that called for the creation of a "United Nations Rapid Deployment Policy and Security Force."

When the summit was over, the Security Council issued a joint declaration approving the strengthening of the UN's peacekeeping ability. The declaration said:

> Bearing primary responsibility under the Charter for the maintenance of international peace and security, the Security Council, in particular its Permanent Members, has an abiding interest in ensuring that the UN is equipped to meet the challenge it faces.[11]

As I thought about this, I was reminded that a rapid deployment force was what the European leaders were asking Javier Solana to create for the EU. In other words, the EU and the UN were doing almost exactly the same thing, and at the same time.

Yet what intrigued me about the UN's plans for strengthening its peacekeeping ability was the fact that it included a religious element—the World Peace Summit. While the world's secular heads of state were attempting to find ways to control the physical side of globalization, the world's religious leaders were attempting to find ways to control the spiritual side of globalization.

The reason this interested me was because of the Bible prophecies. If you recall, in Revelation 13 two beasts are scheduled to come on the scene in the end times. And a beast in Bible prophecy refers to both a king and a kingdom.

The first beast we already learned about—the 10-horned beast from the sea. As you know, I believe the first beast may well be the current revival of the Roman Empire under the European Union. I believe the second beast could well be this reorganized United Nations under some kind of religious control.

Here's another interesting point: In his statement at the beginning of this segment, Tim Lahaye says he believes it's possible the UN could someday move its headquarters to Babylon in modern Iraq. And, in the aftermath of the second Iraqi war, his idea does look conceivable.

However, even if the UN doesn't move its headquarters, there are good reasons for believing the UN may become the second beast from the earth. The second beast has two horns. Horns are prophetic signs of power. In Revelation 13, these horns appear to represent someone who has great economic and religious control over the world. According to the Bible, the second beast will require people to take a mark on their right hand or forehead in order to buy or sell. The mark will be associated with the worship of an image.

And, instead of rising from the sea as the first beast does, this second beast rises from the earth. There are two things that make this interesting to me. One reason is something the Apostle John once said about false prophets. He said, "They are from the world; therefore they speak as from the world, and the world listens to them" (1 John 4:5). And here, in the UN, we have world leaders listening to the clergy who reject the Gospel of Jesus.

Another interesting thing about the second beast rising from the earth is because, from John's perspective on the island of Patmos, Babylon is inland. This further suggests the possibility of this new UN being located in Babylon, Iraq. Again, I'll deal more with this subject and the second Iraqi war later.

Back to the new UN: Do you recall what these anti-Christian religious leaders want to do? They want to establish an International Advisory Council within the UN These world religious leaders want to advise the secular world leaders about ways to achieve global peace.

When you add the plans of these religious leaders to the fact that the world's political leaders are already looking for ways the UN can control the global economy,[12] then the prophecy about people being required to take a mark and worship an image in order to buy or sell doesn't seem so farfetched.

So what does this mean to us? It means that—if the UN is the foretold second beast from the earth—then it will gain control over the economies and the religious rights of all nations. And it also means some very powerful religious leader will soon rise to a place of authority within the UN

As I thought about the Club of Rome's Declaration—what sounds like a declaration of war against the Bible and God's people—and the two UN summits recently held in New York, a passage of Scripture came to my mind. I opened my Bible and read those familiar words from Psalms 2. But this time they had a different meaning:

Why are the nations in an uproar, and the peoples devising a vain thing? The kings of the earth take their stand, and the rulers take council together against the Lord and against His Anointed; 'Let us tear their fetters apart, and cast away their cords from us!' He who sits in heaven laughs, the Lord scoffs at them. Then He will speak to them in His anger and terrify them in His furry; 'But as for Me, I have installed My King Upon Zion, My holy mountain.'"

For the first time, these words from the Old Testament made me shudder. But, they also reassured me. In the end, God will prevail.

Chapter 9 Notes

1. Tim Lahaye, *Revelation: Illustrated and Made Plain*, 101.

2. J. Dwight Pentecost, *Prophecy For Today*, 82.

3. Donella H. Meadows *et al.* (1972) "The Limits To Growth," [abstract by Eduard Pestel] *The Club of Rome*, Internet: http://www.clubofrome.org.

4. To learn more about secular humanism, I recommend David A. Noebel's book, *Understanding the Times* (Eugene: Harvest House Publishing, 1991) ch. 24.

5. The members of the Club of Rome (1996, April 25) "Declaration of the Club of Rome," *The Club of Rome*, Internet: http://www.clubofrome.org.

6. R. F. M. Lubbers and J. G. Koorevarr, "Governance in an era of Globalization," [paper for the Club of Rome Annual Meeting] *Club of Rome*, Internet: http://www.clubofrome.org.

7. Solana (2000, July 7) "Inaugural Conference of the Course 'Towards a New International Morality: the Humanitarian Interventions,'" [speech] *Europa*, Internet: http://www.europa.eu.int.

8. Tim Lahaye, *Revelation: Illustrated and Made Plain*, 242.

9. Austin Ruse (2000, August 30) "Turner Attacks Christianity at UN 'Peace Summit,'" *NewsMax.com*, Internet: http://www.newsmax.com.

10. United Press International (2000, September 7) "World Leaders Call for Change at UN," *Drudge Report*, Internet: http://www.drudgereport.com.

11. United Press International (2000, September 8) "Big Five Back UN 'Reforms,'" *Drudge Report*, Internet: http://www.drudgereport.com.

12. Ibid.

10

Solana's Cool Coup

o o o o o o o o o o o o o o o o o o o o o o o o o o o o o o o o o
*Only the divine interpretation of history and the divine revelation of
the prophetic future of nations can give us a sure light in these trou-
bled days.*[1]

—*John F. Walvoord, 1967*

Just when I began to feel sure I had found the alliance that could soon become
the 10 kings of prophecy, I heard some news that suggested otherwise. I heard a
report that the Western European Union was being dismantled. Associated Press
writer Jeffrey Ulbrich said:

> The Western European Union—the nearly defunct alliance that was briefly
> revived as the military arm of the European Union—began preparations today
> for its likely demise, with foreign and defense ministers organizing the transfer
> of its functions to the European Union.[2]

Was this the end of the 10 Brussels Treaty Powers alliance? If it was, prophetically speaking, I was up a wrong tree. They were not to become the 10 kings of
prophecy after all.

I had known that the European leaders had wanted the EU to take over the
peacekeeping tasks of the WEU for some time. I'd been following the discussions
and knew the future shape of Europe's new military wing was unresolved.

The biggest problem these European leaders seemed to be dealing with had to
do with their plans for enlargement. The 15-nation EU was preparing to grow to
25 nations or more. The question was how such a large number of nations could
democratically participate in the decision-making process of a military alliance
without sacrificing its effectiveness.

One only has to recall how difficult it was keeping all 19 NATO nations together during the bombing campaign against Serbia. Each nation had its own set of targets it wanted hit and set of targets it didn't want to hit. This led to a lot of unnecessary confusion in Allied headquarters and may even have contributed to the accidental bombing of the Chinese Embassy.

On the other hand, the idea of not giving every member state a democratic voice in the EU's military was also unacceptable. Member states couldn't be expected to send their sons and daughters into harm's way without representation. So, some kind of parliamentary body would have to be decided upon to provide this democratic element.

The WEU had already worked out these problems by organizing an assembly, made up of 28 nations—only 10 had full voting rights. Now that the EU was planning on taking over these WEU operations, the system that had been so effective would have to be recreated within the EU.

The European Parliament wanted to be the body that provided this democratic oversight. But until the enlargement process was completed, the European Parliament would only be made up of 15 nations. If the Rapid Reaction Force was ready by their goal of 2003, it would be up and running long before the other 12 candidate nations could have any say in the Parliament.

The other possibility for oversight of the new European military was the WEU Assembly. This parliamentary body was seen as a better choice because it was already made up of 28 nations. The WEU Assembly also had years of effective experience in giving many nations a voice in decisions regarding military matters.

Yet just turning the EU's military wing over to the 28-nation WEU Assembly would violate the primacy of the EU's 15 member states. After all, this was supposed to be the EU's military.

But dealing with the lack of democracy wasn't the only problem the EU would have to work out before it could take over the functions of the WEU. Article five of the modified Brussels Treaty still linked 10 nations together in a mutual defense agreement that could not be set aside or given to another organization.[3] In other words, under the existing treaties, the EU leaders couldn't completely do away with the WEU, no matter how badly they wanted to.

Besides, I was suspicious: If those 10 Brussels Treaty Powers that controlled the WEU were, in fact, to become the 10 kings of prophecy, then they wouldn't be giving up their relationship to each other so easily. Although there may be talk about breaking them up, it wouldn't happen.

Yes, things in Europe were getting complicated. When I stumbled across the Maastricht Treaty (effective 1993), I found that it didn't call for the elimination of the WEU. Instead, it specified that the WEU would be the "armed force" that was to be used by the EU.[4]

But the leaders of the EU wanted more than just their own military machinery. They also wanted someone to run it for them. So in the Amsterdam Treaty (effective May 1999), the EU nations called for the creation of a new office of High Representative for the Common Foreign Security Policy (CFSP). This is an office Javier Solana currently holds. They also decided to transfer all military decision-making away from the WEU to the Council of the European Union and their new High Representative.

The Council has its headquarters in Brussels in the Justus Lipsius building. This building contains the office of the Council Secretary General and High Representative, posts currently held by Javier Solana. It also houses the Legal Service agency and 10 more agencies known as Directorates.

Then, in December 1999, the Helsinki European Council took even more away from the WEU organization. It called for new political and military bodies to be established within the Council of Europe headquarters in Brussels, to duplicate those that existed in the WEU.

In other words, the political and military bodies within the 10-nation WEU alliance were to be eliminated and duplicated within the Council of Europe.

It was no wonder people were thinking the WEU was being done away with. But, in reality, this was not the case. As I said before, the elimination of the WEU would cause treaty problems that would take time for the EU leaders to work out. Those 10 nations still had their responsibility to each other under Article Five of the modified Brussels Treaty.

When I considered the huge tasks before the EU leaders—creating an effective decision-making process, eliminating the democratic deficit, preserving the primacy of the 15 member states, and maintaining the obligation of the 10 Brussels Treaty Powers—I didn't see how they were going to do it. Yet these matters would all have to be resolved before their Rapid Reaction Force was ready in 2003. To me, their assignment seemed impossible.

Evidently, the EU leaders were also worried. So this is how they decided to deal with their dilemma. They called for temporary political and military bodies to be set up until all those difficult problems could be worked out. In the meantime, they wanted these interim bodies operational by March 2000. The new temporary bodies were to assist the Council in making recommendations and carrying out the daily operations of their new military wing until the permanent bodies were in place.

In other words, for the time being, Solana was to direct the EU's new military wing from his Brussels office without any parliamentary oversight. And this dangerous lack of democracy would exist until the EU heads of state could figure out what to do about it.

So Solana went right to work establishing these new interim political and military bodies within his Council of Europe headquarters. And, sure enough, the Political and Security Committee held its first meeting on March 1, 2000. It was made up of ambassadors and senior officials of the member states. The next week, the military body held its first meeting. It was made up of military representatives of the member states. Then on March 8, Solana appointed Brigadier Graham Messervy-Whiting as the head of these military experts. Once again, Solana was doing his job well.

Now the fate of the WEU seemed uncertain. Its head (the decision-making element) had been severed from its body (the WEU Assembly) and a new head (the Political and Security Committee) was being created for it in the Council of Europe. From now on, the missions fulfilled by the WEU—the so-called "Petersberg tasks" (peacekeeping and peacemaking)—would become the responsibility of Solana and the Council of Europe.

Yet, as I said before, the Amsterdam Treaty didn't call for the complete elimination of the WEU. The treaty did, however, allow for the possible integration of the WEU into the EU. But once the WEU had been integrated, it was to continue its life within the EU.

So the Associated Press writer, Jeffrey Ulbrich, said that the WEU had begun preparations for its demise. No doubt this is what Brussels had officially said. But the Brussels officials have a habit of doing what they say they're not. They say they're not creating a European army, but they are. They say they're not weakening the NATO alliance, but they are. They say they're not creating a new power center with the office of High Representative, but they are.

Despite everything they say, I knew something for sure. If the 10 Brussels Treaty Powers were to become the 10 kings of Bible prophecy, then they would somehow end up staying together. Not only that, but if they were to be those kings, then the relationship between them and the office of High Representative would continue to grow closer and stronger. And this is exactly what happened.

The Devil's in the Details

o o o o o o o o o o o o o o o o o o o o o o o o o o o o o o o o o o

It (the Antichrist) very well could be some individual who is known as an international leader, someone whose true nature and character is not suspected; one to whom all the world will look as a deliverer, and never dream that this one will so give himself to the control of Satan that he will become the 'little horn,' 'the king of fierce countenance,' or, 'the prince that shall come,' the 'abomination of desolation,' 'the lawless one,' or 'the Beast.' [5]

—*J. Dwight Pentecost, 1961*

On July 1, 2000, France took over the six-month rotating presidency of the EU and the Council of the European Union. If you recall, the Council is the main decision-making body in the EU. Now one of the 10 Brussels Treaty Powers held the presidency of the EU. Immediately under the French presidency, the Council announced its decision to make the WEU Assembly the temporary assembly for Europe's new military wing. The WEU Assembly was renamed the "Interim European Security and Defence Assembly." So, the 10 Brussels Treaty Powers were still together—and they were in charge of managing Europe's new military.[6]

This was what I was expecting to happen. I never believed the 15-nation European Parliament was going to get the job of managing Europe's new military. The 28-nation WEU Assembly was, by far, the best choice if the EU leaders wanted to give every nation a voice in the military decision-making process.

And for the time being, this firmly locked the 10 Brussels Treaty Powers in place since only they had full voting rights in this Assembly. The 10 nations I had been watching had just had their monopoly on Europe's new military wing guaranteed. And to this day, they remain in charge of the military.

Then something else happened that frightened a lot of people. It was called the "Solana Decision." But before I tell you about the Solana Decision, I must explain something. This is because the politics in the EU can be very confusing.

The EU is actually built around five institutions. Through a series of treaties, the 15 nations that make up the EU give portions of their governmental responsibilities to these institutions. Of these institutions, three are considered the most powerful. These three are referred to as the "institutional triangle"—the European Parliament, the Council of the European Union, and the European Commission. Only one of these institutions is made up of democratically elected officials—the European Parliament. The other two are made up of appointed officials.

The Council of the European Union is the main decision-making body within the EU. This concerns many citizens in Europe because, as I said, the Council is made up of unelected officials. Many citizens believe this creates a dangerous lack of democracy in the EU since the only representation they have is in the European Parliament.

Now that I've explained a little about these three EU institutions, I can tell you about the Solana Decision. On July 26, 2000, quickly following the French presidency's decision to use the WEU Assembly for their military, Solana called a meeting of COREPER (committee of permanent representatives of the 15 member states). Strangely, he called this meeting while the European Parliament was in recess. Not only that, but he didn't inform the national parliaments of the 15 member states about this meeting or any civil organizations.[7]

At the meeting, Solana put forward a resolution restricting the public's access to all documents relating to military matters. It was quickly voted on and passed. In other words, from now on any actions by Solana and the Council of Europe regarding Europe's new military wing was going to be hidden behind closed doors.

Not only was the public affected by this decision, but it also left the European Parliament—the only democratic element in the EU's institutional triangle—completely in the dark. Even more serious, the Solana Decision reversed a commitment made in the Amsterdam Treaty guaranteeing the public's right to these same documents. Without this guarantee, it's doubtful if the parliaments of the 15 member states would have ratified the Amsterdam Treaty in the first place.

This clampdown on public access to information became known as the infamous "Solana Decision." Some journalists even went so far as to call it Solana's "military coup."[8]

Needless to say, the actions of the French presidency and the Solana Decision angered and alarmed the European Parliament. They felt that—without their right to military documents—they couldn't provide the democratic oversight they were responsible to their citizens for. And they didn't trust the WEU Assembly to do the job since only the 10 Brussels Treaty Powers had full voting rights.

A dangerous lack of democracy was being institutionalized inside the EU's new foreign and security policy. The EU's military wing was falling completely into the unelected hands of the Council of Europe. And the 10 Brussels Treaty

Powers were maintaining their exclusive military monopoly. And this is the situation today.

I began to suspect that something big was going on in the EU just below the surface. The 10 Brussels Treaty Powers held the majority in the 15-nation EU. I realized that, if these 10 nations worked together in the Council of Europe, then they could do just about anything they wanted.

Evidently I wasn't the only one who suspected something questionable might be going on. In fact, these events began a war in the EU—a press release war. For a while, I couldn't keep up with all the opposing press releases coming from the different institutions.

The European Parliament fired the first shot. They countered the actions of the French Presidency and the Solana Decision. In draft reports submitted on October 6 and 16 of 2000, the Parliament called for the modified Brussels Treaty to be denounced and for the WEU and its Assembly to be abolished. In other words, they wanted to break up the 10 Brussels Treaty Powers.

This was something the Brussels Treaty Powers obviously didn't want to happen. The WEU Assembly quickly responded by saying:

> The European Parliament is well aware that the collective defence cannot become a task for the European Union in the medium term and that the WEU member countries cannot therefore denounce the modified Brussels Treaty in the foreseeable future. Indeed, our Governments have no intention of so doing.[9]

Then the Netherlands fired their salvo. To the surprise of the other EU member states, the Netherlands filed a lawsuit in the European Court of Justice against the Solana Decision. Sweden and Finland gave their support to the Dutch. Interestingly, these were the only three EU nations that voted against Solana in the Council meeting on the day his decision was adopted.[10]

It goes without saying that the Euro-skeptics—the civil liberties organizations and other groups concerned with the free flow of information throughout the EU—were all going completely bananas.

Then on November 13, 2000, with the end of the six-month French presidency in sight, the Brussels Treaty Powers delivered their nuclear bomb—the Marseille Declaration. This decision once again reaffirmed these 10 nation's relationship under the Modified Brussels Treaty and called for maintaining the WEU for this very purpose.

But the reason I called the Marseille decision a nuclear bomb was because it eliminated all but the10 Brussels Treaty Powers from the new decision-making process. In other words, now the democratic deficit in the new military wing would be complete.[11]

Although these 18 other nations never had the same full voting rights as the 10, they did play a big roll in the WEU assembly. Now, since all crisis management decisions would be the responsibility of the Council of Europe, they no longer had a voice. This is when the EU's new military wing fell under the sole control of Solana and the 10 Brussels Treaty Powers. From then on, there's been no democratic oversight in the EU's fledgling military.

The reason the Council of Ministers gave for excluding these 18 nations from the decision-making process was because of the EU's plans for enlargement. According to them, once these nations were integrated into the EU they would again "have their place at the table." In the meantime, the 10 Brussels Treaty Powers and the Council of Europe would enjoy complete control over the EU's military.

I couldn't help but think about how these 18 other nations in the WEU Assembly had recently spoken out in defense of the 10 Brussels Treaty Powers when the European Parliament called for their demise. This was the way they were rewarded. Now they had been excluded from the decision-making process by the same 10 nations they had defended.

But no one seemed to be catching on. The next day, on November 14, the AP news wire reported, "The Western European Union went out of business without a whimper Monday, after 52 years of biding time on the sidelines of history."

Yet, on December 5, Solana delivered a speech to the same WEU Assembly that supposedly had gone out of business. He said:

Looking forward to the moment when the EU assumes direct responsibility for crisis management, ministers in Marseille decided on the functions and structures which would remain with WEU. Clearly, the modified Brussels Treaty and the mutual defense commitment contained in its Article V are the raison d'etre for maintaining WEU. The reaffirmation in Marseille by the member states of that commitment is recognition that it remains an important underpinning for their other European and Atlantic engagements.[12] In other words, the final decision about the shape of the EU's new military wing had been made under the French presidency. The WEU would continue, but in a much smaller and more controllable arrangement. It would be stripped of everything that wasn't necessary for Solana and the 10 Brussels Powers to maintain control of Europe's exclusive military club.

As I thought about all these events in last six months of 2000, I was reminded of the mandate the EU leaders gave to Solana. His job was to create a military and civilian crisis management capacity for the EU by 2003. But he was only given until the end of 2000 to work out all of the details. This explained why so much had happened during the last six months of the year 2000. With the help of the French presidency, Solana was working out those details.

That the French presidency would play such a pivotal role in finalizing the details about the EU's military wing should have come as no surprise. France has championed the creation of a European superstate from the beginning. And to become a superstate, you need an army. In fact, many Europeans trace the beginning of the EU to the "Schuman Declaration"—a proposal by French Foreign Minister Robert Schuman. On May 9, 1950, he suggested the establishment of the European Coal and Steel Community. Schuman proposed this move as the first step in creating a European federation. Today Europeans recognize May 9 as Europe Day—the day the EU began.

So where was America during all these events that took place in the EU during the last half of 2000? All eyes in America were glued to Florida. The wildly fluctuating election results coming in between Al Gore and George W. Bush were keeping the American public on the edge of their seats. It was the closest presidential election in modern history. The American news networks were consumed with hanging chads, uncounted ballets, and legal options available to the candidates.

No one in the American media seemed to notice what was taking place in Europe. Even if they had noticed, it was doubtful they could have understood it. They would have simply dismissed the political events occurring in Europe as they would events on some remote island.

Even for someone like me who had been watching, this flurry of events in the EU was hard at first to understand. Double-talk and contradictions flow from Brussels like biblical milk and honey. The account I've provided in this book has come from bringing together many loose pieces of information.

Yet in confusing times like these, Bible prophecy can come to our aid. The Apostle Peter calls prophecy "a lamp shinning in a dark place" (2 Peter 1:19). It doesn't provide us with all the details, but it does tell us where these events in Europe are ultimately going. They are headed toward a seven-year security agreement between the revived Roman Empire and Israel—an agreement destined to be broken.

So I had my own understanding about what was going on in the EU. And my idea was quite different from what the officials in Brussels were saying. I recall thinking to myself, "The EU isn't absorbing the WEU; Solana and the 10 Brussels Treaty Powers are absorbing the EU."

Solana's Agenda

o o o o o o o o o o o o o o o o o o o o o o o o o o o o o o o

This world ruler when he comes to authority in the European federation of nations will look over to Palestine and see that the Arab-Israeli dispute threatens world peace.[13]

—*J. Dwight Pentecost, 1961*

o o o o o o o o o o o o o o o o o o o o o o o o o o o o o o o

He will pose as a great humanitarian, the friend of men, and the especial friend of the Jewish race, whom he will persuade that he has come to usher in the 'Golden Age' as pictured by the prophets, and who will receive him as their Messiah.[14]

—*Clarence Larkin, 1920*

My suspicion that the stage was being set for the rise of the Antichrist was becoming overwhelming. I decided to pay even closer attention to what Solana was saying. On November 14, 2000, Solana summed up his accomplishments to date as High Representative in a speech given to the German Foreign Affairs Association in Berlin.[15] After a few words of introduction, Solana began his speech by saying:

> The past year has been a time of major innovation in the area of the Union's Common Foreign and Security Policy. Every European Council has proved to be a new high-water mark in extending the range of instruments available under the Common Foreign and Security Policy and moving towards a more effective, more coherent and more visible Foreign Policy.

After reminding his listeners that the world problems would not wait for the EU to get their foreign policy in order, he asked his audience three questions: "Are we willing to deliver? Are we capable of delivering? And have we delivered in the course of the last year?" Then he answered his own questions. The most interesting answer, however, was probably the first. Regarding the EU's willingness to deliver, he said:

> There is now a serious commitment to presenting a single political will to the rest of the world, a commitment to match Europe's economic power with political influence. This is the enormous change, which we have witnessed in Europe over the last year. The creation of the post of High Representative itself was an indication of this new willingness by the member states of the Union to make CFSP work.

Solana's words were hauntingly familiar to me. Here he referred to a "single political will" and making the EU's new Common Foreign Security Policy (CFSP) work. According to the Bible, this is the relationship the Antichrist is to have with the 10 kings. If you recall, referring to the Antichrist, the angel told John:

> For God has put it in their [the 10 kings] hearts to execute His purpose by having a common purpose [CFSP], and by giving their kingdom to the beast [High Representative for the CFSP], until the words of God should be fulfilled (Revelation 17:17). [Words in brackets are my own]

Also in answer to his first question, "Are we willing to deliver?", Solana said, "CFSP is about Europe making a difference in international politics. It is about the European Union being able to project its values and its interests—the core of its political identity—effectively beyond its own borders."

When I saw the words "core of its political identity," I couldn't help but wonder if there was a deeper meaning that many might not catch. Could Solana have been alluding to a hidden political agenda of certain core nations within the EU?

In his speech, Solana also said the EU needed to focus its new foreign policy where it was most needed. The first area it was needed was in regard to the EU's neighbors—the surrounding European nations. He said this was why the enlargement process was so important. At the time of his speech, 12 new nations had applied for membership in the EU.

Yet he wasn't just thinking about the current round of candidates. Solana went on to include other candidates by adding: "Within the same fold, the countries of the Balkans and the Southern Mediterranean shore deserve our utmost attention."

In other words, he wanted to someday admit Israel into the EU. Yes, there seems to be no way around it. Solana's Mediterranean foreign policy could place him, and the European heads of state he has been working with, right smack in the middle of end-times Bible prophecy. If Solana were to succeed with these plans, the EU would indeed be a true revival of the Roman Empire.

At the time of this speech the Middle East had become a hot spot. In September 2000, violence had broken out in Israel when Ariel Sharon visited the Temple Mount in Jerusalem. The riots that began that day on the Temple Mount in Jerusalem spread across all of Israel and soon the American-sponsored peace process had completely collapsed. Now Palestinian leader Yasser Arafat was appealing to the European Union to come in and protect them from the Israeli army, and Solana was itching to get involved.

So, in his speech, Solana began talking about the Middle East. He said:

> A few weeks ago I was asked by EU foreign ministers to travel to the region to meet all the parties concerned and to try to offer support in the search for an end to the violence. The rounds of talks I held in the region paved the way for participation by the European Union in the Sharm el-Sheikh summit, which allowed us for the first time to be actively involved in the search for a solution to the crises…I have been nominated by President Clinton and UN Secretary General Kofi Annan to become a member of the fact-finding Commission set up in Sharm-el-Sheikh. I will continue to work in support of the search for peace in the Middle East; the European Union will continue to be fully engaged.

Amazing. Now Solana had managed to secure a place for himself on the fact-finding Commission that had been set up to find a way to bring an end to the violence in the Middle East. Here he was just beginning his job as Mr. Europe and he was already positioning himself to be the one to bring peace to Israel. These are all things the foretold Antichrist is supposed to do.

By the time I had finished reading Solana's speech, I was convinced that the recent events in the Mediterranean and Europe were prophetic road signs indicating that the end-times prophecies were about to be fulfilled. And once again, no one seemed to be noticing.

Chapter 10 Notes

1. John F. Walvoord, *The Nations in Prophecy*, preface.

2. Jeffrey Ulbrich, "Euro Union Set for Its Own Demise," *The Associated Press*, Oporto, Portugal, Monday, May 15 2000; 3:48 a.m. EDT.

3. European Union *(1954, October 23)* "Protocol Modifying and Completing the Brussels Treaty," *Europa*, Internet: http://www.europa.eu.int.

4. European Union (1991) "Maastricht Treaty," *Europa*, Internet: http://www.europa.eu.int.

5. J. Dwight Pentecost, *Prophecy For Today*, 91.

6. Western European Union (2000, June 8) "France aims to preserve WEU-ESDA role as 'forum,'" [press release] *WEU Assembly*, Internet: http://www.weu.int.

7. Deirdre Curtin, "Authoritarian Temptation Seduces EU Decision-makers," *Statewatch News Online*, Internet: http://www.statewatch.org.

8. Ibid.

9. Western European Union (2000, October 26) "WEU Assembly rejects European Parliaments call to denounce the modified Brussels Treaty" [press release] *WEU Assembly*, Internet: http://www.weu.int.

10. See note 7 above.

11. Western European Union (2000, December 5) "WEU-ESDA Assembly calls on WEU Ministers" [press release] *WEU Assembly*, Internet: http://www.weu.int.

12. Javier Solana (2000, December 5) "Address by the WEU Secretary General to the WEU Assembly—(Paris)" [speech] *Europa*, Internet: http://www.europa.eu.int.

13. J. Dwight Pentecost, *Prophecy For Today*, 84.

14. Clarence Larkin, *Dispensational Truth*, 122.

15. Javier Solana (2000, November 14) "Where does the EU stand on Common Foreign and Security Policy—Forschungsinstitut der Deutschen Gesellschaft fuer Auswaertinge Politik—Berlin" [speech] *Europa*, Internet: http://www.europa.eu.int.

11

The Second Overlooked Sign: Recommendation 666

o o o o o o o o o o o o o o o o o o o o o o o o o o o o o o o o

You would like me to tell you what 666 means, wouldn't you? I have to confess that I don't know. But I am certain that there are more than 666 interpretations as to what is meant! This was written for the benefit of those who will be alive in that day. And believers in the Lord Jesus Christ in the day of the manifestation of the man of sin will have a very clear identifying sign that the one that has come to world power is Satan's great masterpiece.[1]

—*J. Dwight Pentecost, 1961*

Yet how could I be sure of something like this? How could I know that the 10 Brussels Treaty Powers were, in fact, becoming the 10 kings of Bible prophecy? How about Javier Solana? Could he actually be the first to hold the office the Antichrist is soon going to hold?

Some Christians would laugh at such questions. And I don't blame them. Under normal circumstances I would laugh, too. But they haven't followed the trail I've followed since the end of the Gulf War.

They may not understand that we could actually see the beginning of the Antichrist's kingdom before the rapture of the church and the return of Christ (see Chapter 1, Misconception 6). And they haven't been told about all the events that occurred in Europe during the last six months of 2000. Even if they had, they may not realize their relevance to the prophecies.

Yet back to that first question. How could I be sure? Even after all the events I witnessed that indicate the prophecies may be soon fulfilled, I could still be wrong. You see, Bible prophecy wasn't given to us so we can predict the future.

God placed prophecies in His Word so that, when the events predicted are fulfilled, we'll believe. Although it may appear to me that the prophecies are about to be fulfilled, this may prove not to be the case. And if that happens, I'll look like a fool. Of course, it wouldn't be the first time.

Even after all my careful research and Bible study, I could find that I've been following a convincing, but dead-end trail. As I said at the beginning of this book, Christian history is filled with this type of thing occurring. And it doesn't only happen to false brethren—sometimes it happens to the sincere.

The idea that I could be reading things into these events really began to frighten me. I could see myself as another misguided prophecy teacher leading others down another prophetic dead-end path. I began to question everything about myself—my column, my motives, everything. Many times I'd asked God to keep me from error. Now I was asking Him again.

I was becoming so convinced that I was witnessing the prophecies being fulfilled that it scared me. And the idea that I could actually know what the office of the Antichrist might be seemed totally ridiculous.

So I prayed until peace returned to my heart. When the peace came, I knew it didn't mean I was right about the prophecies. It only meant that I had given my problem to God. And He would answer me in His time.

After praying, I turned to a document from the WEU Assembly Web site that I hadn't had time to read. It was document #C/1720—a report submitted by the Political Committee about the future role of the WEU.[2] I began reading and underlining the parts that had to do with the 10 Brussels Treaty Powers and the office of High Representative.

I noticed a recommendation regarding the office Solana occupied. It had something to do with making the High Representative "sufficiently strong." I wondered what this meant.

That's when I saw it. It was in a paragraph under the heading "Introduction and Summary." In the first sentence it read, "Nearly five months from the adoption of Assembly Recommendation 666 on the consequences of including certain functions of the WEU in the European Union...."

I almost fell from my chair. I couldn't believe what I was looking at. It was that infamous number of prophecy, 666! And it had something to do with what had just occurred in the EU.

I hurried to my computer and downloaded the document. It was Assembly document #A/1689.[3] And there it was. At the top of the page in large red print it said "Recommendation 666." Below this, in smaller print, it continued, "on the consequences of including certain functions of the WEU in the European Union—reply to the annual report of the Council."

But what did it mean?

The first thing I had to do was calm myself down. After all, this had been quite a trip. First it had been the discovery of the WEU alliance back in 1991. Then it was the meaning of that election in Israel in 1992. In 1995, the WEU officially became 10 nations, and a new office of High Representative was created in 1999. Then, in the last six months of 2000, I saw these 10 nations and the High Representative gain control of the EU's new military alliance. Now I was looking at a WEU document that was somehow connected with these prophetic events—and it was titled Recommendation 666.

I knew this might be very significant. From what I could see, the document was a reply to the annual report of the Council by the WEU Assembly. And it didn't seem to be saying anything new. Once again, it suggested maintaining the relationship between the10 Brussels Treaty Powers. It said:

> Take the measures necessary for the WEU to ensure that the collective defense commitment provided for in Article V of the modified Brussels Treaty is effectively maintained, taking account of the recent decisions concerning the European Security and Defense Policy.

Nothing appeared new, that is, until I got to the 12th recommendation in the document. Apparently, the WEU Assembly was recommending that the already powerful offices that Solana holds be made even stronger. It said:

> Support proposals for the WEU Secretary-General and the CFSP High Representative to preside over the PSC and civilian crisis-management machinery and give him powers to convene the Council of the European Union in the event of an emergency.

These were all posts held by Solana. The PSC is the Political and Security Committee. This is one of the decision-making interim bodies that Solana had created in the Council of Europe headquarters. The WEU Assembly was recommending that Solana be made head over this agency also.

Not only that, but it also was suggesting that Solana be given the powers to convene the Council of Europe in the event of an emergency. At first I didn't understand the significance of this last part of the Recommendation. I knew it had to do with the chain of events that occurred under the French presidency in the last six months of 2000. The Recommendation was adopted June 5,

2000—just before the beginning of the French presidency. So the French presidency was acting on Recommendation 666 when it announced its decision to make the WEU Assembly the Interim European Security and Defense Assembly. They were also following it when they decided to maintain the relationship between the 10 Brussels Treaty Powers.

It is also possible the Recommendation led to the Solana Decision—the infamous decision to clampdown on the public's right to military documents. It must have been behind the exclusion of those other 18 nations from the crisis management decision process as well.

But there was something more here—something I hadn't quite placed my finger on. Then it finally dawned on me what Recommendation 666 really meant. And it was at that moment—when I finally understood the implications of the Recommendation—that I knew I had to write this book.

The officials in Brussels were using the word "interim" to describe the new military bodies they had created. As we have learned, the new military structure they had decided upon under the French presidency is only supposed to be temporary. Yet I began to realize there was something in Recommendation 666 that could make it permanent.

Number 12 of the Recommendation suggested that the High Representative be given something extraordinary. In the event of an emergency, the High Representative has the authority to step in and take control of the EU's new military machinery. One would think such powers would be reserved for the EU presidency.

As I thought about this, I realized the stage may now be set for the rise of the Antichrist. If a big enough crisis were to occur before the dangerous democratic deficit that now exists in the EU's military wing is resolved, then the High Representative could step in and evoke his emergency powers given to him by Recommendation 666.

Could this emergency authority be part of a humanist strategy to bring about world government? It sure could. In fact, well-known humanist Edith Wynner said the only way a humanist world government could be established is by granting emergency powers to some authority. She said, "Our present tragic necessity requires that world government begin with massive emergency authority granted for ten to twenty years."[4]

The idea struck me. Should Solana, or some future High Representative, ever step in and take power in such a manner—and create some kind of dictatorship—this person's rise to power would be associated with the number 666. And if this person's authority were to become global, as J. Dwight Pentecost said, we would have a "very clear identifying sign that the one that has come to world power is Satan's great masterpiece."[5]

Later, I would arrive at a clearer understanding of the prophetic significants of what happened in July 2000. This was when a 10-nation alliance was officially made the military wing of the EU. And, this is when the EU began on a course of competing with America for control of the Mediterranean.

Interestingly, this change in the EU's foreign policy ultimately did lead to the confrontation between the US and the EU that Carlos Masala had warned about in his essay. In February 2003, for the first time in modern history, France and Germany shocked the world and openly opposed the United States in the UN Security Council over a resolution for a second Iraqi war

This major shift in the EU's foreign policy began when the 10-nation alliance adopted their Western European Union Assembly Recommendation 666.

And, this event could actually mark the beginning of the rise of the foretold 10-horned beast from the sea.

Truth or Coincidences?

o o o o o o o o o o o o o o o o o o o o o o o o o o o o o o o o
Here is wisdom. Let him who has understanding calculate the number of the beast, for the number is that of a man; and his number is six hundred and sixty-six.[6]

—Apostle John, A.D. 54–96

This brings us to a significant question: Was it a coincidence that the number 666 was used to identify a recommendation that could someday be linked with a man's rise to power with 10 nations and a revived Roman Empire? Perhaps it was.

I went back to my computer and downloaded Assembly Recommendations 664 through 670. I wanted to see if these documents could be equally interpreted to implicate these 10 Brussels Treaty nations as the possible 10 kings of Bible prophecy and Solana's office of High Representative as the future office of the Antichrist.

They didn't. Recommendation 664 dealt with recommendations regarding the parliamentary dimension of the EU's new military. Recommendation 665 had to do with the associate members. Recommendation 665 had to do with the

18 associate nations, not the10 Brussels Treaty nations. Recommendation 667 was concerned with certain WEU budget matters.[7]

Recommendation 666 was the only document that made recommendations regarding continuing the relationship of the 10 Brussels Treaty Powers and giving more power to the office of High Representative.

This brought me to an interesting question. After 2,000 years of speculation on this number in prophecy, could I have finally stumbled upon its meaning? I reread where this number is mentioned in the Bible. The Apostle John said, "Here is wisdom. Let him who has understanding calculate the number of the beast, for the number is that of a man; and his number is six hundred and sixty-six" (Revelation 13:18).

"Calculate" indicates counting numbers. I wondered if the Greek word John used here, *psephizo*, had a broader meaning. It did. In fact, this is the only place in the New Testament this word is found.

Strong's Exhaustive Concordance reveals something interesting. It gives the meaning of this Greek word this way: "to use pebbles in enumeration." It also says this is from another Greek word, *psephos*. This word means "a pebble, as worn smooth by handling. A counter or ballot. A verdict." And this word is from even another Greek word, *pselaphao*, meaning "to manipulate, verify by contact. To search for; feel after, handle, touch." So the Greek word translated as "calculate" doesn't just mean to count as in "one-two-three." At the time the Apostle John wrote these words, pebbles were used to calculate numbers in much the same way as we use our modern computers. So the word "calculate" refers to something more like the operation of a modern computer.

I'm no computer expert. But one thing I do know is that computers simply process numbers. People who work with computers say that computers "crunch numbers." That's why we call the brain of a computer a microprocessor. From the way I understand it, the computer chip is a huge bundle of miniaturized, electrical, on-off switches. The electric current flows through the chip according to these switches, depending on if they are turned on or off. If there's no error in the chip, and the computer has been programmed correctly—meaning all the switches have been set right—then it will always come to the right answer.

Getting back to the number 666. The Bible tells us to calculate the number. And the Greek word means "to calculate using pebbles." Many don't realize that the computer has been in existence, in one fashion or another, since ancient times. The only difference is that today's computers are capable of processing bigger numbers, and they are much faster.

From this we could infer that—if we have arranged all our pebbles in the right order and have followed them precisely—then we will arrive at a certain answer, just like a computer.

But, where, or what, are the pebbles we are to use in our calculations? To answer this question, we must go back and look at the verse again. The angel of Revelation said, "Here is wisdom. Let him who has understanding calculate the number of the beast."

So where, or what, are our pebbles? Since our subject matter is Bible prophecy, I believe our pebbles are all those little nuggets of prophecies that have been scattered throughout the Scriptures—from the foretold "seed of the serpent" in Genesis to the glorious return of Christ in the book of Revelation.

Now I'll share with you what I suspect the number could mean. If we have correctly understood the prophecies—in other words, if we have placed all the pebbles in the right order and if we follow them precisely—then we will, when the time comes, arrive at the person who is to be associated with that number. And that number is 666.

Chapter 11 Notes

1. J. Dwight Pentecost, *Prophecy For Today*, 99.

2. Western European Union (2000, November 15) "The implementation of the Common European Security and Defense Policy and WEU's future role—reply to the annual report of the Council," [report] Document C/ 1720, *WEU Assembly*, Internet: http://www.weu.int.

3. Western European Union (2000, May 10) adopted 5 June, "The consequences of including certain functions of WEU in the European Union—reply to the annual report of the Council," [report] Document A/ 1689, *WEU Assembly*, Internet: http://www.weu.int.

4. David A. Noebel, *Understanding the Times*, 582.

5. Pentecost, *Prophecy For Today*, 99.

6. *New American Standard Bible*, Revelation 13:18.

7. These documents can be found on the WEU Assembly Web site: http://www.weu.int.

12

9/11 and the Beast From the Earth

o o o o o o o o o o o o o o o o o o o o o o o o o o o o o o

men fainting from fear and the expectation of the things which are coming on the world; for the powers of the heavens will be shaken [1]

—*Jesus*

If the first beast of Bible prophecy is to be born from events associated with Recommendation 666, then it is likely the second beast could be born from the world changing events of September 11.

Here's why I believe this: Sometimes we focus so much of our attention on the first beast described in the 13th chapter of Revelation that we forget there is a second beast. Unlike the first 10-horned beast that comes from the sea, the second beast has only two horns and comes from the earth. [2]

This second beast—later called the False Prophet—is a powerful religious figure who will direct worship toward the first beast. This second beast will also cause all people, both rich and poor, to receive a mark on their right hand or forehead in order to buy or sell. And, if you recall, a beast in Bible prophecy is a king and his kingdom that rises over Israel.

Here's my point: This religious figure will need some kind of kingdom to enforce his global religious and economic control. I believe his kingdom will be the United Nations. And I believe America may play a big role in bringing his kingdom about.

Picture yourself on the island of Patmos where the Apostle John had his visions of these two beasts. This small island is off the coast of what is today known as Turkey.

We already know that the first beast John saw coming from the sea was Rome. And, from John's perspective, Rome was in the direction of the sea. This being the case, it follows that the second beast John saw coming from the earth could mean some inland kingdom (from John's perspective), like Iraq.

The reason I'm pointing this out is that, since the first Gulf War, I've been expecting American forces to occupy Iraq. And now that they are, it looks like America and the UN will share the job of nation building and managing Iraq's enormous oil wealth.

No matter what people thought about the Iraqi war, the balance of power in the Middle East has changed forever. With American and international forces at their doorstep, the Middle East nations will have to learn how to live in harmony with their new, powerful neighbor. And this includes Israel.

In other words, in the aftermath of September 11 and the Iraqi war, I believe America and the UN will create the end-times Babylon of Revelation. And it is this Babylon that the Antichrist and the 10 kings will destroy in one hour at the end of the tribulation.[2]

What does September 11 have to do with all this? For the first time in history, America experienced an attack on her home soil. And, like the rising smoke from the inferno where once stood the Twin Towers of the World Trade Center, America roused herself for her new war—a war against terror.

This war would have two fronts. One front would be on America's homeland. It would be fought with new, almost draconian-style security measures. The other front would be anywhere in the world. It would be fought with pre-emptive military engagements.

At first the European leaders seemed to agree with Washington's reaction to September 11. And NATO, for the first time in the alliance's history, evoked the mutual defense clause in their treaty. This meant that the September 11 attack on America was considered an attack on all 19 member states of the North Atlantic Treaty Organization.

However, the Europeans didn't feel as threatened by the events of September 11 as did the Americans. So when President Bush called Iran, North Korea and Iraq an "axis of evil," some of the European leaders became concerned. Later, when the Bush administration revealed its plans to go to war in Iraq, these European leaders turned their concern into direct opposition. This opposition would ultimately lead old allies into the deepest and most damaging spats in modern history.

Although the official spin was that the Europeans who opposed the Iraqi war did so because they thought it would set a dangerous precedent and violate international law, I saw it differently. I saw their opposition as part of the EU's new war with the United States over control of the Mediterranean—a war that began with the implementation of Recommendation 666.

You see, an American-led war in Iraq would also mean a long-term presence of American forces in the Middle East. And this was something these European leaders didn't want. Why? Because, if you recall, the EU leaders had their own plans for the region—the Euro-Mediterranean Partnership.

But, thanks in a large part to September 11, America would go to war in Iraq. And what the European leaders who opposed the war feared would happen, happened. American forces would go to war and remain, giving America and the UN a large, permanent footprint in the Middle East.

So the events of September 11 may have set the stage for the second beast from the earth to appear—the False Prophet and the Babylon of prophecy.

Now here is where it gets interesting. As I said before, the prophecies tell us the 10 kings and the Antichrist will hate this Babylon and destroy her in one hour with fire. With the way the European nations who implemented Recommendation 666 now appear to hate the United States over Iraq, it's not hard to see how this event could happen.

However, there is another reason they will hate this Babylon. The Bible tells us God will put it into the hearts of the 10 kings and the Antichrist to have a common foreign policy—His foreign policy—to want to destroy this end-times Babylon (Revelation 17:16–17).

Why will God do this? Because this Babylon killed His people who refused to receive the mark. And this Babylon divided up His land Israel (Revelation 19:2, Jeremiah 50:24, Joel 3:1–2).

Yes, the end-times stage is being set. But few are noticing.

Getting the Message Out

My journey discovering Recommendation 666 had been an exciting ride. Getting the story out, however, would prove to be even more exciting.

On January 1, 2001, Sweden took over the EU presidency for the next six-months. Unlike France, Sweden wasn't a member of Javier Solana's 10-nation military alliance. If I was right about Solana's alliance becoming the 10 kings of prophecy, then the fast-paced fulfillments of the prophecies I had witnessed under the prior French presidency would slow down. In July, however, things could speed up again. At that time Belgium—another member of Solana's alliance—would take Sweden's place at the EU presidency. In other words, under the Swedish presidency there could be a lull in the fulfillment of the prophecies that would provide a six-month window in which I could write this book.

I needed such a window—a period without too much happening in the EU because I knew I wouldn't be able to keep up with the political events in Europe and write a book at the same time. Yet even while immersed in my writing, interesting news continued to come about Solana.

On May 8, just as my book was beginning to take shape, the results of the Mitchell Report were released. As you may recall, former Senator George Mitchell was tasked with heading a committee to find a way to stop the continuing violence in the Israeli/Palestinian conflict. President Bill Clinton asked Solana to have a seat on Mitchell's committee.

The findings were as I suspected. The committee put the blame for the violence equally on Israel. The report ignored the fact that the violence began entirely with the Palestinians and continued under the direct control of Palestinian leader Yasser Arafat. And, of course, the committee also called for a freeze on all new Israeli settlements.

As I said before, September 11 changed our world in a big way. But the shattering effect of that day wasn't only to our world's sense of peace and security. It also had a devastating effect on the global economy—especially here in America. In fact, I'd soon learn the events of September 11 would even have a negative effect on the publication of this book. When the economy goes south, so does book sales.

By October, I had finished my first manuscript and was waiting for a reply from several publishers. In the meantime, the events I had written about that appeared to be fulfillments of prophecy continued to unfold in Europe. And, as always, it frustrated me that nobody was noticing.

Yet another amazing encouragement from God was on its way. That October, I attended the Bakersfield Business Conference. This conference is unlike any other business conference in the world. The speakers aren't just ordinary people. Each year the speakers include many former heads of state and top celebrities.

Coming just a month after September 11, the security at the conference was the highest I'd ever seen. Not only were metal detectors in use at all the gates, but plain-clothed officers were strolling around the grounds with assault rifles.

Each year I attend the conference I have the same strange thought. I wonder if this time I'll be able to speak to one of the key players in our world about the things I wrote my book about—the possible fulfillments of prophecy in Europe and Israel. This time, not only did I get to speak with someone important, but I was able to speak with one of the key players I had written about—former Secretary of Defense William Cohen.

Naturally, I wanted to know what Cohen thought about the EU's new military wing created by Javier Solana and the French presidency. As I said before, Cohen once warned the EU heads that, if they created an independent military command, NATO would become a "relic of the past."

So I asked Cohen about this. Now that the EU leaders had gone ahead and done what he had advised against, will NATO become a relic of the past?

Cohen looked me in the eye and said, "In my opinion it hasn't happened."

His answer startled me. I knew better than that. After all, I had written an entire book about the EU creating their own independent military. My face must have revealed what I was thinking because Cohen decided he needed to reply more in depth. And, in so doing, I was about to be provided with a piece of inside information that would become very valuable in the days to come.

Cohen again looked me in the eye and said, "What the EU leaders have done is only for show—they only want the European people to think they have their own independent military."

At the time I didn't understand the implications of what Cohen said. Now, however, I do. Evidently, at the time I asked him the question (October 2001), Cohen still believed the EU's new military command structures were only for show. So apparently, when the concerned Clinton administration approached Solana and the EU heads about what they had done by implementing Recommendation 666, they were assured that the EU's new military structures were just for show. And the Clinton administration bought it.

By December 2001, my hope for getting my book published was fading. A year had passed since my discovery of Recommendation 666 and my book still wasn't going anywhere. All those old doubts were returning to my head. Was what I wrote about really a fulfillment of prophecy? Was it really God's will for me to write a book?

Needless to say, that Christmas morning my mood wasn't quite as joyous as the rest of my family. When the gifts were passed, I received an envelope from a family member with what I assumed would be a gift certificate. But when I opened it, I had the shock of my life. It was a gift certificate that declared, "You're the proud owner of FulfilledProphecy.Com."

In other words, I now had my own Web site.

FulfilledProphecy.Com

o o o o o o o o o o o o o o o o o o o o o o o o o o o o o o

And this gospel of the kingdom shall be preached in the whole world for a witness to all the nations, and then the end shall come.[3]

—*Jesus*

In February 2002, my new Web site, FulfilledProphecy.Com, appeared on the World Wide Web. Soon it had a faithful following. People were coming back daily to keep up with the news and read commentaries about how the news could relate to Bible prophecy.

By the end of July 2003, FulfilledProphecy.Com was averaging over three thousand hits a day and that number was growing faster each month.

The first edition of this book was also available for purchase on my Web site as an eBook. However, the most important information contained in this book was posted on my Web site for free.

Thanks to my unusual gift on that gloomy Christmas day, the world would finally learn about Recommendation 666.

Chapter 12 Notes

1. Luke 21:26

2. Revelation 17:16–18

3. Matthew 24:14

13

The Bottom Line

As for me, I heard but could not understand; so I said. 'My Lord, what will be the outcome of these events?' And he said, 'Go your way, Daniel, for these words are concealed and sealed up until the end time. Many will be purged, purified and refined; but the wicked will act wickedly, and none of the wicked will understand, but those who have insight will undersatand[1]

—*The Angel Gabriel, 6th century B.C.*

Does this mean I have uncovered the meaning of the number 666? Will the Antichrist someday come into power by evoking the emergency powers given to him by Assembly Recommendation 666? Does this mean those 10 Brussels Treaty Powers are to become the 10 kings of prophecy, and the office Javier Solana holds will someday belong to the Antichrist?

I truly don't know. Like J. Dwight Pentecost said at the beginning of the chapter eleven, this could be the 667th interpretation of that mysterious number. And it could prove to be just as wrong as all the others. We'll just have to wait and see.

What I do know is events are occurring that appear to be fulfilling the end-times prophecies. Things are happening like the dispensational scholars have said. And this could mean that the Antichrist and his kingdom are soon to appear on the world scene.

But I also realize I could be wrong like so many sincere students of Bible prophecy who have come before me. Yet, even if I am wrong, there is an important lesson to be learned by the events I have talked about in this book.

Someday these end-times events that Jesus warned us to watch for will occur. And when they do, they may happen in a way we don't expect—in a place where we're not looking. As in the days in which Jesus appeared to Israel, we may be waiting for the Messiah but looking for the wrong signs.

And once again, Jesus will come at a time when we least expect.

Last Call?

○ ○

Therefore, take up the full armor of God, that you may be able to resist in the evil day, and having done everything stand. Stand firm therefore, having girded your loins with the truth, having put on the breastplate of righteousness, and having shod your feet with the preparation of the Gospel of peace. [2]

—*Apostle Paul, A.D. 62*

So now that I've shown you how events may be occurring in Europe and the Mediterranean that appear to be fulfilling the end-times prophecies, what does it all mean for us? Before I answer this question, I'll start by saying what it does not mean. It does not mean the events I've shared with you are, for certain, fulfillments of the end-times prophecies. Their fulfillment could still be many years away.

And it doesn't mean you should take my opinions about Bible prophecy and build your faith around them. I could be wrong, in part, or in all. But if it turns out I am wrong, it doesn't mean the prophecies have failed. Someday all the end-times events predicted in the Bible will occur exactly as written.

In the meantime, we students of prophecy need to remember two things. First, the images in Bible prophecy have an on-going nature. And, second, the wicked spiritual forces attempting to bring the Antichrist and his kingdom on the scene were already beginning their work at the time of the Apostle John.

These two facts make it easy for sincere Bible students to mistakenly see events occurring in their day as fulfillments of prophecy. And this could be the case with the recent events in Europe and the Mediterranean. In other words, I could be jumping the gun.

Now I will tell you what these events do mean. They mean that you and I had better be ready. There's a chance I'm not jumping the gun. The end-times events predicted in Bible prophecy—that terrible time period referred to as "the day of the Lord"—could soon spring upon the world like Jesus said, as a "thief in the night."

The question now before us is: When the day of the Lord begins who will survive? According to the Apostle Paul, in order for us to survive, we must be prepared. Paul warns, when that terrible time begins it may be already too late (2 Thessalonians 2:11–12). He said that to survive the day of the Lord will require special armor. We will need to be wearing what he calls "the full armor of God." He said:

Therefore, take up the full armor of God, that you may be able to resist in the evil day, and having done everything stand. Stand firm therefore, having girded your loins with the truth, having put on the breastplate of righteousness, and having shod your feet with the preparation of the Gospel of peace (Ephesians 6:13–14). The first part of our armor is to gird our loins with the truth. This means, if you're not a believer in Jesus, then you need to become one. Jesus said, "I am the way, and the truth, and the life; no one comes to the Father, but through Me" (John 14:6).

But before we can come to Jesus for salvation, we must first recognize something. In God's eyes, we are all sinful and guilty of death. If you don't think you're guilty of sin, tell me which of God's 10 commandments have you not broken? Have you never told a lie? Have you never coveted something that belonged to another or taken something that was not yours? The Bible clearly tells us that we all are guilty of sin: "for all have sinned and fall short of the glory of God" (Romans 3:23).

The Bible also clearly tells us that, by our own merits, we are not pure enough to stand before a Holy God and survive. The Apostle Paul wrote, "There is none righteous, not even one; there is none who understands, there is none who seeks God; all have turned aside, together they have become useless; there is none who does good, there is not even one" (Romans 3:10–12).

Yet it is in this hopeless condition we find our hope. The fact that we have together all "become useless" means that all of us—no matter how bad or good we think we are—have exactly the same chance before God. Because we're all under sin, we are all eligible for His great salvation. About this hope, the Apostle Paul said:

For while we were still helpless, at the right time Christ died for the ungodly.
For one will hardly die for a righteous man; though perhaps for the good man someone would dare even to die, but God demonstrated His own love toward us, in while we were yet sinners, Christ died for us (Romans 5:6–8).

So, how does the Bible say we can take advantage of this hope? Paul answers this question. He said:

But what does it [Scripture] say? 'The word is near you, in your mouth and in your heart'—that is the word of faith which we are preaching, that if you confess with your mouth Jesus as Lord, and believe in your heart that God raised Him from the dead, you shall be saved; for with the heart man believes, resulting in righteousness, and with the mouth he confess, resulting in salvation. For the Scripture says, 'Who ever believes in Him [Jesus] will not be disappointed '(Romans 10:8–11).

When we have come to believe in Jesus, and that we are all sinners and that Jesus died for our sins, we have put on the first part of our armor—we have girded our loins with the truth.

Now we need to put on the second part of our armor—the breastplate of righteousness. Just knowing what to believe isn't enough. We must act on our belief and begin creating a genuine relationship with Jesus. We must accept, by faith, His forgiveness for our sins. And we must begin living a life that is pleasing to Him. This means that when we stumble back in sin—and we very well may—we immediately go back to Him and confess our sin and start over. When we've believed in Jesus for the forgiveness of our sins and have turned from our former sinful life, then we have put on the breastplate of righteousness.

And there is one more important part to our armor we must not forget—we must shod our feet with the preparation of the Gospel of peace. This means we need to always be willing, at a moment's notice, to leave this world behind for the sake of Christ and His kingdom. We need to be always ready to go and preach His Gospel message, and we need to be ready for His return.

To have this attitude requires us to guard our hearts. We need to always make sure that our treasures are in heaven and not on earth. When we have this disposition, we have on the third part of our armor and are ready for the day of the Lord.

You see, a lot of people today will tell you they know God. But on the day of the Lord, what will only count is if God knows them (Galatians 4:9, 2 Timothy 2:19).

Are you ready for the day of the Lord? (Have you put on the full armor of God?) Have you girded your loins with the truth? (Do you believe you are a sinner and that Jesus died in your place?) Have you put on the breastplate of righteousness? (Do you have a real relationship with Jesus and have you turned from your sins?) Are your feet shod with preparation of the Gospel of peace? (Are you willing, on a moment's notice, to leave this world behind for Jesus and His kingdom?)

If not, now is the time to put on the full armor of God. If you wait too long, it may be too late and you'll have to face the terrible day of the Lord without it.

This could be the last call.

"And behold, I am coming quickly [suddenly]. Blessed is he who heeds the words of the prophecy of this book [who is ready]". [3]

Jesus, approximately A.D. 95

Chapter 13 Notes

1. Daniel 12:8–10

2. Ephesians 6:13–14.

3. Revelation 22:7

Epilogue

And The Beat Goes On

February 28, 2002: The Convention on the Future of Europe held its inaugural meeting. The European Council tasked the Convention with creating a constitution for the new, super EU due on the scene in 2004. And a constitution, of course, means the birth of a nation state. In this case, however, it was a rebirth—a rebirth of the old Roman Empire.

March 12, 2002: The United Nations Security Council passed Resolution 1397. The resolution called for the creation of a Palestinian state. And to everybody's amazement, it was sponsored by Israel's closest friend—America. Officially, both Washington and Jerusalem said nothing changed. But words couldn't hide the obvious—the long-standing united American-Israeli front in the Security Council had finally been broken.

July 1, 2002: The International Criminal Court (ICC)—the first world court—became operational. Only 60 nations were needed to ratify the Rome Statute treaty that called for the creation of the ICC. One report I read stated that with 60 nations needed, the treaty was ratified with 66—6 more than needed. In other words, the writer went out of their way to report the numbers associated with this historic event in a way that would link it to that infamous number of prophecy–666.

September 12, 2002: Valéry Giscard D'Estaing, president of the Convention on the Future of Europe, said the role of the EU's foreign policy chief, Javier Solana, should be enhanced. Giscard said Solana's office should have a seat on the European Council, alongside the EU heads and president of the Commission. In other words, if Giscard's proposal is accepted, the person who holds Solana's office would become as powerful in the new EU as a member state.

October 7, 2002: The European Parliament and the Council finally came to an agreement on the infamous Solana Decision. As you may recall, in July 2000, the

Solana Decision put a stop to public access of Council documents of military nature. Three EU member states took the Solana Decision to court. Now an agreement has been reached. A limited number of individuals will be allowed access, but only to information the Council approves. In other words, this decision is a victory for the Council and Solana.

January 1, 2003: Greece, one of the 10 WEU nations, took over the EU six-month rotating presidency. And on July 1, Italy, another WEU nation, took over the EU presidency from Greece. Why is this interesting? For one thing, this order—Greece followed by Italy (Rome)—is the same order of Gentile kingdoms we find foretold in the book of Daniel that will rise to rule over Israel (Daniel 2:31–45, 10:20–21, 9:26). Furthermore, at the end of the Greek presidency the EU had its summit. And this summit was held in the Greek city of Thessaloniki. Ironically, it was also to the Christians in Thessaloniki that Paul sent his two most in-depth letters in the New Testament concerning the coming Antichrist. Could this be a warning?

February 14, 2003: France and Germany surprised the world with an apparent coordinated action in the UN to block Washington's and London's request for a new Security Council resolution authorizing force in Iraq. Here's how it happened: On January 16, chief UN weapons inspector, Hans Blix, held talks with European officials—including Solana. On February 5, U.S. Secretary of State Colin Powell delivered his evidence to the Security Council of Iraqi obstruction to the inspections. On February 8, France, Germany and Belgium kept NATO from providing protection to Turkey. Then, on the 14th, after Blix unexpectedly shot down Powell's evidence, France and Germany voted down Washington's and London's request for a resolution. They called it Operation Mirage.

March 20, 2003: The United States and Great Britain began their invasion of Iraq. The war was begun without UN approval, and against the wishes of most EU leaders—including four of the 10 WEU member states. However, three WEU members states—Britain, Spain and Portugal—split from the pack and held their own mini-summit to show solidarity with the United States. In other words, rejecting the EU's new foreign policy that began with Recommendation 666, they supported American's vital interests in the Mediterranean instead. This event, and the one that follows, led me to wonder if these could end up being the three kings destined to be subdued by the coming Antichrist in his rise to power.

April 29, 2003: France, Germany, Belgium, and Luxembourg held their own mini defense summit. These were the four WEU member states that opposed the Iraqi war. Their goal was to create a so-called "hard core" group of nations within the EU who would not always support American interests over Europe's. In other words, these four WEU member states wanted to eliminate the three pro-American states from their group. Although Javier Solana didn't attend the meeting, he made it clear he supported the idea of a hard core group.

June 13, 2003: The draft constitution for the new, super EU was officially presented to the Convention. Besides making the EU a legal personality, the constitution called for a longer-term EU president and a powerful new foreign minister. This foreign minister will have a seat in the Council next to the member states and have the ability to make and sign treaties. Ironically, the day Giscard chose to present his constitution was Friday the 13th.

June 19, 2003: Javier Solana presented his 10-page security doctrine to the EU heads at their June summit. On June 25, at the EU/US summit held in Washington, Solana, the EU heads and the Bush administration signed an important agreement to coordinate their efforts in the fight against terror and weapons of mass destruction. When the EU and the US came together in this new treaty, it was as if two great beasts settled their differences by agreeing to divide up the prey. And, the deal was made possible by Solana's new security doctrine. I've included my commentary about this event. It's also posted on my Web site at: www.fulfilledprophecy.com.

Solana's Secure Europe and Better World

The most amazing thing is happening. Just last week, the fragile world order lay fractured and nobody knew what to do about it. Now, suddenly, a man may have appeared with a solution.

Here was the problem: The Iraqi war was threatening to turn old friends into new enemies. Some EU member states—such as Germany, France and Belgium—strongly and openly opposed America going to war in Iraq. Others—such as Britain, Spain and Portugal—fully supported the war. Then there were all the remaining EU nations, on both sides of the Iraqi issue, who also had strong feelings but stayed out of the fight.

To make matters worse, an unusual heat wave awaited the EU heads when they gathered in Greece for their important June summit. At this summit, the

EU heads would be tackling the most difficult and controversial issues over what shape their new, super EU would take.

This was the setting for the EU's High Representative, Javier Solana, to present his 10-page document. It was titled, *A Secure Europe in a Better World.* And, its goal was to give the EU a new foreign policy that would achieve what its name implied.

Solana's plan had three basic parts. First, it called for the EU to contribute more resources to establishing economic and political stability in their neighborhood. Second, it called on the EU to build an international order. And third, it called for the EU to strengthen its civil and military capacity to deal with the threat of weapons of mass destruction and rogue states.

There was nothing really surprising about Solana's plan. What was surprising was the way everybody loved it. France loved it because it would create a multipolar world to counter American dominance. Germany loved it because it would build an international order. Britain, Spain, Portugal and the 10 new EU members loved it because it stressed the importance of maintaining good relations with America and the Atlantic alliance. Even the United States liked this part.

Another thing that interests me is the timing. Solana couldn't have delivered his proposal at a better time. As I mentioned before, the EU heads were discussing the blueprint for their new EU. And part of this blueprint called for a much more powerful EU foreign minister who will have a seat in the Council next to the heads of state. Not only that, this new foreign minister will also have the authority to sign treaties for the EU. In other words, as far as foreign policy goes, whoever holds this new foreign minister post could end up being more powerful than even the new EU president.

Like I said, just last week the fragile world order lay fractured and nobody knew what to do about it. Now, suddenly, a man may have appeared with a solution.

If I were looking for a foreign minister, I know who I'd choose.

Stay tuned!
www.fulfilledprophecy.com

Look among the nations! Observe!
Be astonished! Wonder!
Because I am doing something in your days—
You would not believe if you were told.[5]

God, between 650 B.C. and 330 B.C.

About the Author

For more than 10 years, Herb Peters' weekly religion columns have appeared in several California newspapers. His timely columns and commentaries have been circulated widely in print and on the Internet. Herb is also the founder and owner of the popular Web site on Bible prophecy, FulfilledProphecy.Com (www.fulfilledprophecy.com).

The importance of Bible prophecy is something Herb knows first-hand. In fact, it was because of a book on prophecy that he became convinced the Bible was true and became saved more than 30 years ago. This explains his passion for prophecy and why he has so diligently studied the subject since his conversion.

Herb owns and operates an insurance agency he established in 1974. He and his wife, Linda, have been married for 32 years and attend a Baptist church.

0-595-28871-5

Printed in the United States
30211LVS00005B/403-411